TEACHER'S PET PUBLICATIONS

PUZZLE PACK
for
The Adventures of Tom Sawyer
based on the book by
Mark Twain

Written by
William T. Collins

© 2005 Teacher's Pet Publications
All Rights Reserved

The materials in this packet are copyrighted
by Teacher's Pet Publications, Inc.

These pages may be duplicated by the purchaser
for use in the purchaser's own classroom.

Copying any of these materials and distributing them
for any other purpose is a violation of the copyright laws.

© 2005 Teacher's Pet Publications, Inc.
www.tpet.com

INTRODUCTION
If you already own the LitPlan for this title, this Puzzle Pack will refresh your Unit Resource Materials and Vocabulary Resource Materials sections plus give you additional materials you can substitute into the tests. If you do not already have a complete LitPlan, these pages will give you some supplemental materials to use with your own plan. There are two main groups of materials: one set for unit words (such as characters' names, symbols, places, etc.) and one set for vocabulary words associated with the book.

WORD LIST
There is a word list for both the unit words and the vocabulary words. These lists show you which words are being used in the materials and the clues or definitions being used for those words. You may want to give students a word list with clues/definitions to help them, or you may want students to only have a word list (without clues/definitions) if you want them to work a little harder. Both are available for duplication. The word lists can also be your "calling key" for the bingo games.

FILL IN THE BLANK AND MATCHING
There are 4 each of the fill in the blank and matching worksheets for both the unit and vocabulary words. These pages can be used either as extra worksheets for students or as objective parts of a unit test. They can be done individually if students need extra help or as a whole class activity to review the material covered.

MAGIC SQUARES
The magic squares not only reinforce the material covered but also work on reasoning and math skills. Many teachers have told us that their students really enjoy doing these!

WORD SEARCH PUZZLES
The word search words go in all directions, as indicated on your answer keys. Two of the word search puzzles have the clues listed rather than the words. This makes the puzzle a little more difficult, but it reinforces the material better. Two word search puzzles have words only for students who find the clue puzzles too difficult.

CROSSWORD PUZZLES
Both unit and vocabulary word sections have 4 crossword puzzles.

BINGO CARDS
There are 32 individual bingo cards for the unit words and 32 individual bingo cards for the vocabulary words. You can use your word list as a "call list," calling the words at random and marking them off of your list as you go, or you could use the flash cards by cutting them apart and drawing the words at random from a hat (or box or whatever). To make a better review, you might ask for the definition and spelling of each word as you call it out–or you could call out the definitions and have students tell you the words they need to look for on the puzzle.

JUGGLE LETTERS
The vocabulary juggle letter game is intended to help students learn the spellings of the words. One sheet has the definitions listed on it as an extra help for students who need it or to reinforce the definitions if you choose to do so.

FLASH CARDS
We've included a set of vocabulary flash cards you can duplicate, cut, and fold for your students. Some teachers make a few sets for general use by the class; others make a set for each student. Some teachers duplicate them for each student and have the students cut & fold their own. You can cut out just the words and put them in a hat, have each student pick out one word and write the definition and a sentence for that word. Students then swap words and papers, with the next student adding a sentence of his own under the last one. You can have students swap as many times as you like. Each time the student will read the sentences written prior to his own and then add a sentence. You can cut out the words and definitions separately and play "I Have; Who Has?" Each student in the room draws a word and definition. The first student says, "I have (the name of the word). Who has the definition?" The student with the definition reads it then says, "I have (the name of the vocabulary word she has). Who has the definition?" The round continues until all words and definitions have been given.

Tom Sawyer Word List

No.	Word	Clue/Definition
1.	ALFRED	New boy; spilled ink on Tom's book
2.	AMY	Tom had been engaged to her before Becky.
3.	BARK	Tom's notepaper
4.	BECKY	She was engaged to Tom.
5.	BOOK	Becky tore the teacher's
6.	CANDLE	Tom blew out Becky's to conserve.
7.	CATS	Dead ones are good for curing warts.
8.	CAVE	Place where Tom and Becky got lost
9.	CLEMENS	AKA Twain
10.	CONSCIENCE	Tom brought things to Muff Potter to ease his ___.
11.	COURT	Place where the trial is held
12.	CUFFS	Tom got these and kisses from Aunt Polly upon his return.
13.	DOBBINS	The teacher
14.	DOUGLAS	The widow
15.	FENCE	Tom was supposed to whitewash it
16.	FINN	Huck's last name
17.	FISH	Food for island boys
18.	FUNERAL	The boys attended their own
19.	GANG	Group of boys; Tom Sawyer's ___
20.	HOUSE	Haunted ___
21.	HUCK	Son of the town drunk
22.	INJUN	Murderer: ___ Joe
23.	INK	It spilled on Tom's spelling book.
24.	JACKSON	___'s Island
25.	JOE	Went to island with Huck and Tom
26.	KNIFE	A gory one was found next to Dr. Robinson
27.	MARY	Tom's girl cousin
28.	MISSISSIPPI	The river
29.	MURDER	What Tom and Huck witnessed in the graveyard
30.	NEWSPAPER	Tom's name was printed in it for telling on Injun Joe
31.	PAIN	Tom gave some to Peter, making him act crazy: ___ killer
32.	PETER	The cat
33.	PINCHBUG	Tom passed time in church by watching this.
34.	PIRATES	They wore fancy clothes.
35.	POLLY	Tom's guardian
36.	POTTER	Muff; drunk accused of murder
37.	ROBINSON	Doctor Injun Joe killed
38.	SAWYER	Tom's last name
39.	SID	Tom's half-brother
40.	SKIFF	Small boat
41.	SMOKE	Huck taught Tom & Joe how to do this bad habit.
42.	SPADE	The boys left it and the pick downstairs.
43.	SPIT	Tom could do this through the gap in his teeth.
44.	PETERSBURG	Tom's town: St. ___
45.	THATCHER	Becky's last name
46.	TICKETS	Ten yellow ones were redeemed for a Bible.
47.	TOE	Tom had a sore one.
48.	TOM	He took the blame for tearing the teacher's book.
49.	TRADED	How Tom got his tickets
50.	TRAPPED	Injun Joe got ___ in the cave and died.
51.	TREASURE	You have to dig for it where the shadow of a dead tree limb falls at

		midnight.
52.	TWAIN	Author
53.	TWO	Number __
54.	WALTERS	Sunday school superintendent
55.	WELSHMAN	He saved Widow Douglas.
56.	WIG	The boys stole Mr. Dobbins's
57.	WITCHES	Tom blamed the unsuccessful marble spell on these.
58.	WITNESS	Tom was one to Dr. Robinson's murder.

Tom Sawyer Fill In The Blanks 1

_____ 1. He saved Widow Douglas.

_____ 2. Tom had a sore one.

_____ 3. Murderer: ___ Joe

_____ 4. Place where the trial is held

_____ 5. The teacher

_____ 6. Tom had been engaged to her before Becky.

_____ 7. Small boat

_____ 8. Tom brought things to Muff Potter to ease his ___.

_____ 9. ____'s Island

_____ 10. The boys stole Mr. Dobbins's

_____ 11. Huck taught Tom & Joe how to do this bad habit.

_____ 12. Haunted ___

_____ 13. You have to dig for it where the shadow of a dead tree limb falls at midnight.

_____ 14. Tom got these and kisses from Aunt Polly upon his return.

_____ 15. Son of the town drunk

_____ 16. The widow

_____ 17. Doctor Injun Joe killed

_____ 18. Tom was one to Dr. Robinson's murder.

_____ 19. What Tom and Huck witnessed in the graveyard

_____ 20. Tom's guardian

Tom Sawyer Fill In The Blanks 1 Answer Key

WELSHMAN	1. He saved Widow Douglas.
TOE	2. Tom had a sore one.
INJUN	3. Murderer: ___ Joe
COURT	4. Place where the trial is held
DOBBINS	5. The teacher
AMY	6. Tom had been engaged to her before Becky.
SKIFF	7. Small boat
CONSCIENCE	8. Tom brought things to Muff Potter to ease his ___.
JACKSON	9. ___'s Island
WIG	10. The boys stole Mr. Dobbins's
SMOKE	11. Huck taught Tom & Joe how to do this bad habit.
HOUSE	12. Haunted ___
TREASURE	13. You have to dig for it where the shadow of a dead tree limb falls at midnight.
CUFFS	14. Tom got these and kisses from Aunt Polly upon his return.
HUCK	15. Son of the town drunk
DOUGLAS	16. The widow
ROBINSON	17. Doctor Injun Joe killed
WITNESS	18. Tom was one to Dr. Robinson's murder.
MURDER	19. What Tom and Huck witnessed in the graveyard
POLLY	20. Tom's guardian

Tom Sawyer Fill In The Blanks 2

_____ 1. Tom blamed the unsuccessful marble spell on these.

_____ 2. Tom's half-brother

_____ 3. ____'s Island

_____ 4. She was engaged to Tom.

_____ 5. Number __

_____ 6. The widow

_____ 7. Tom had a sore one.

_____ 8. Tom's girl cousin

_____ 9. Injun Joe got ___ in the cave and died.

_____ 10. How Tom got his tickets

_____ 11. Murderer: ___ Joe

_____ 12. Muff; drunk accused of murder

_____ 13. They wore fancy clothes.

_____ 14. Small boat

_____ 15. Author

_____ 16. Went to island with Huck and Tom

_____ 17. He saved Widow Douglas.

_____ 18. He took the blame for tearing the teacher's book.

_____ 19. Tom's last name

_____ 20. Sunday school superintendent

Tom Sawyer Fill In The Blanks 2 Answer Key

WITCHES	1. Tom blamed the unsuccessful marble spell on these.
SID	2. Tom's half-brother
JACKSON	3. ____'s Island
BECKY	4. She was engaged to Tom.
TWO	5. Number __
DOUGLAS	6. The widow
TOE	7. Tom had a sore one.
MARY	8. Tom's girl cousin
TRAPPED	9. Injun Joe got ___ in the cave and died.
TRADED	10. How Tom got his tickets
INJUN	11. Murderer: ___ Joe
POTTER	12. Muff; drunk accused of murder
PIRATES	13. They wore fancy clothes.
SKIFF	14. Small boat
TWAIN	15. Author
JOE	16. Went to island with Huck and Tom
WELSHMAN	17. He saved Widow Douglas.
TOM	18. He took the blame for tearing the teacher's book.
SAWYER	19. Tom's last name
WALTERS	20. Sunday school superintendent

Tom Sawyer Fill In The Blanks 3

1. Tom's notepaper
2. Food for island boys
3. Dead ones are good for curing warts.
4. Injun Joe got ___ in the cave and died.
5. It spilled on Tom's spelling book.
6. Number __
7. Tom was supposed to whitewash it
8. ____'s Island
9. Huck's last name
10. Muff; drunk accused of murder
11. She was engaged to Tom.
12. What Tom and Huck witnessed in the graveyard
13. The boys left it and the pick downstairs.
14. Tom's girl cousin
15. New boy; spilled ink on Tom's book
16. The boys attended their own
17. AKA Twain
18. Doctor Injun Joe killed
19. Small boat
20. He took the blame for tearing the teacher's book.

Tom Sawyer Fill In The Blanks 3 Answer Key

BARK	1. Tom's notepaper
FISH	2. Food for island boys
CATS	3. Dead ones are good for curing warts.
TRAPPED	4. Injun Joe got ___ in the cave and died.
INK	5. It spilled on Tom's spelling book.
TWO	6. Number __
FENCE	7. Tom was supposed to whitewash it
JACKSON	8. ____'s Island
FINN	9. Huck's last name
POTTER	10. Muff; drunk accused of murder
BECKY	11. She was engaged to Tom.
MURDER	12. What Tom and Huck witnessed in the graveyard
SPADE	13. The boys left it and the pick downstairs.
MARY	14. Tom's girl cousin
ALFRED	15. New boy; spilled ink on Tom's book
FUNERAL	16. The boys attended their own
CLEMENS	17. AKA Twain
ROBINSON	18. Doctor Injun Joe killed
SKIFF	19. Small boat
TOM	20. He took the blame for tearing the teacher's book.

Tom Sawyer Fill In The Blanks 4

1. The river
2. Becky's last name
3. Author
4. Tom's half-brother
5. Tom's name was printed in it for telling on Injun Joe
6. Tom passed time in church by watching this.
7. The boys attended their own
8. They wore fancy clothes.
9. He saved Widow Douglas.
10. The widow
11. Tom's guardian
12. It spilled on Tom's spelling book.
13. Tom was one to Dr. Robinson's murder.
14. Number ___
15. Huck's last name
16. Small boat
17. Tom gave some to Peter, making him act crazy: ___ killer
18. You have to dig for it where the shadow of a dead tree limb falls at midnight.
19. Tom's notepaper
20. Doctor Injun Joe killed

Tom Sawyer Fill In The Blanks 4 Answer Key

MISSISSIPPI	1. The river
THATCHER	2. Becky's last name
TWAIN	3. Author
SID	4. Tom's half-brother
NEWSPAPER	5. Tom's name was printed in it for telling on Injun Joe
PINCHBUG	6. Tom passed time in church by watching this.
FUNERAL	7. The boys attended their own
PIRATES	8. They wore fancy clothes.
WELSHMAN	9. He saved Widow Douglas.
DOUGLAS	10. The widow
POLLY	11. Tom's guardian
INK	12. It spilled on Tom's spelling book.
WITNESS	13. Tom was one to Dr. Robinson's murder.
TWO	14. Number __
FINN	15. Huck's last name
SKIFF	16. Small boat
PAIN	17. Tom gave some to Peter, making him act crazy: ___ killer
TREASURE	18. You have to dig for it where the shadow of a dead tree limb falls at midnight.
BARK	19. Tom's notepaper
ROBINSON	20. Doctor Injun Joe killed

Tom Sawyer Matching 1

___ 1. CONSCIENCE   A. Haunted ___
___ 2. WALTERS   B. She was engaged to Tom.
___ 3. CAVE   C. Tom passed time in church by watching this.
___ 4. HOUSE   D. Author
___ 5. NEWSPAPER   E. Tom had a sore one.
___ 6. MARY   F. Food for island boys
___ 7. PETER   G. The boys attended their own
___ 8. TWAIN   H. Tom's town: St. ___
___ 9. TOE   I. A gory one was found next to Dr. Robinson
___ 10. TRAPPED   J. He took the blame for tearing the teacher's book.
___ 11. AMY   K. The boys left it and the pick downstairs.
___ 12. PIRATES   L. Tom had been engaged to her before Becky.
___ 13. TICKETS   M. Place where the trial is held
___ 14. FUNERAL   N. Huck taught Tom & Joe how to do this bad habit.
___ 15. TOM   O. Tom's girl cousin
___ 16. PETERSBURG   P. They wore fancy clothes.
___ 17. BECKY   Q. Place where Tom and Becky got lost
___ 18. PINCHBUG   R. How Tom got his tickets
___ 19. SPADE   S. Tom's guardian
___ 20. COURT   T. The cat
___ 21. SMOKE   U. Injun Joe got ___ in the cave and died.
___ 22. FISH   V. Sunday school superintendent
___ 23. TRADED   W. Tom brought things to Muff Potter to ease his ___.
___ 24. POLLY   X. Ten yellow ones were redeemed for a Bible.
___ 25. KNIFE   Y. Tom's name was printed in it for telling on Injun Joe

Tom Sawyer Matching 1 Answer Key

W - 1.	CONSCIENCE	A. Haunted ___
V - 2.	WALTERS	B. She was engaged to Tom.
Q - 3.	CAVE	C. Tom passed time in church by watching this.
A - 4.	HOUSE	D. Author
Y - 5.	NEWSPAPER	E. Tom had a sore one.
O - 6.	MARY	F. Food for island boys
T - 7.	PETER	G. The boys attended their own
D - 8.	TWAIN	H. Tom's town: St. ___
E - 9.	TOE	I. A gory one was found next to Dr. Robinson
U - 10.	TRAPPED	J. He took the blame for tearing the teacher's book.
L - 11.	AMY	K. The boys left it and the pick downstairs.
P - 12.	PIRATES	L. Tom had been engaged to her before Becky.
X - 13.	TICKETS	M. Place where the trial is held
G - 14.	FUNERAL	N. Huck taught Tom & Joe how to do this bad habit.
J - 15.	TOM	O. Tom's girl cousin
H - 16.	PETERSBURG	P. They wore fancy clothes.
B - 17.	BECKY	Q. Place where Tom and Becky got lost
C - 18.	PINCHBUG	R. How Tom got his tickets
K - 19.	SPADE	S. Tom's guardian
M - 20.	COURT	T. The cat
N - 21.	SMOKE	U. Injun Joe got ___ in the cave and died.
F - 22.	FISH	V. Sunday school superintendent
R - 23.	TRADED	W. Tom brought things to Muff Potter to ease his ___.
S - 24.	POLLY	X. Ten yellow ones were redeemed for a Bible.
I - 25.	KNIFE	Y. Tom's name was printed in it for telling on Injun Joe

Tom Sawyer Matching 2

___ 1. AMY				A. Place where the trial is held
___ 2. JOE				B. Food for island boys
___ 3. WITCHES			C. Tom was supposed to whitewash it
___ 4. MARY				D. Small boat
___ 5. DOBBINS			E. The river
___ 6. JACKSON			F. He took the blame for tearing the teacher's book.
___ 7. FISH				G. Tom's last name
___ 8. MURDER			H. Tom got these and kisses from Aunt Polly upon his return.
___ 9. MISSISSIPPI		I. The teacher
___10. SAWYER			J. Muff; drunk accused of murder
___11. FENCE			K. Tom had been engaged to her before Becky.
___12. ROBINSON			L. ____'s Island
___13. PETERSBURG		M. The boys attended their own
___14. CUFFS			N. Tom passed time in church by watching this.
___15. TRADED			O. Doctor Injun Joe killed
___16. INK				P. It spilled on Tom's spelling book.
___17. COURT			Q. What Tom and Huck witnessed in the graveyard
___18. POTTER			R. Went to island with Huck and Tom
___19. TOM				S. Tom blamed the unsuccessful marble spell on these.
___20. PINCHBUG			T. How Tom got his tickets
___21. CAVE				U. Place where Tom and Becky got lost
___22. SKIFF			V. Tom's girl cousin
___23. FUNERAL			W. The boys stole Mr. Dobbins's
___24. POLLY			X. Tom's guardian
___25. WIG				Y. Tom's town: St. ___

Tom Sawyer Matching 2 Answer Key

K - 1.	AMY	A.	Place where the trial is held
R - 2.	JOE	B.	Food for island boys
S - 3.	WITCHES	C.	Tom was supposed to whitewash it
V - 4.	MARY	D.	Small boat
I - 5.	DOBBINS	E.	The river
L - 6.	JACKSON	F.	He took the blame for tearing the teacher's book.
B - 7.	FISH	G.	Tom's last name
Q - 8.	MURDER	H.	Tom got these and kisses from Aunt Polly upon his return.
E - 9.	MISSISSIPPI	I.	The teacher
G - 10.	SAWYER	J.	Muff; drunk accused of murder
C - 11.	FENCE	K.	Tom had been engaged to her before Becky.
O - 12.	ROBINSON	L.	____'s Island
Y - 13.	PETERSBURG	M.	The boys attended their own
H - 14.	CUFFS	N.	Tom passed time in church by watching this.
T - 15.	TRADED	O.	Doctor Injun Joe killed
P - 16.	INK	P.	It spilled on Tom's spelling book.
A - 17.	COURT	Q.	What Tom and Huck witnessed in the graveyard
J - 18.	POTTER	R.	Went to island with Huck and Tom
F - 19.	TOM	S.	Tom blamed the unsuccessful marble spell on these.
N - 20.	PINCHBUG	T.	How Tom got his tickets
U - 21.	CAVE	U.	Place where Tom and Becky got lost
D - 22.	SKIFF	V.	Tom's girl cousin
M - 23.	FUNERAL	W.	The boys stole Mr. Dobbins's
X - 24.	POLLY	X.	Tom's guardian
W - 25.	WIG	Y.	Tom's town: St. ___

Tom Sawyer Matching 3

___ 1. ROBINSON   A. Group of boys; Tom Sawyer's ___
___ 2. SPADE   B. They wore fancy clothes.
___ 3. WITNESS   C. The boys left it and the pick downstairs.
___ 4. FUNERAL   D. Number __
___ 5. TWO   E. The boys stole Mr. Dobbins's
___ 6. TOM   F. He saved Widow Douglas.
___ 7. SID   G. Tom was one to Dr. Robinson's murder.
___ 8. PAIN   H. Place where the trial is held
___ 9. CAVE   I. Tom's notepaper
___10. HUCK   J. Place where Tom and Becky got lost
___11. POLLY   K. The boys attended their own
___12. WIG   L. The cat
___13. TREASURE   M. Tom gave some to Peter, making him act crazy: ___ killer
___14. CUFFS   N. You have to dig for it where the shadow of a dead tree limb falls
                            at midnight.
___15. SKIFF   O. Tom's guardian
___16. SMOKE   P. He took the blame for tearing the teacher's book.
___17. GANG   Q. Tom got these and kisses from Aunt Polly upon his return.
___18. BARK   R. Small boat
___19. COURT   S. Tom could do this through the gap in his teeth.
___20. PIRATES   T. Tom blew out Becky's to conserve.
___21. WELSHMAN   U. Tom's half-brother
___22. CANDLE   V. Son of the town drunk
___23. SPIT   W. Huck taught Tom & Joe how to do this bad habit.
___24. PETER   X. Doctor Injun Joe killed
___25. FINN   Y. Huck's last name

Tom Sawyer Matching 3 Answer Key

X - 1.	ROBINSON	A. Group of boys; Tom Sawyer's ___
C - 2.	SPADE	B. They wore fancy clothes.
G - 3.	WITNESS	C. The boys left it and the pick downstairs.
K - 4.	FUNERAL	D. Number __
D - 5.	TWO	E. The boys stole Mr. Dobbins's
P - 6.	TOM	F. He saved Widow Douglas.
U - 7.	SID	G. Tom was one to Dr. Robinson's murder.
M - 8.	PAIN	H. Place where the trial is held
J - 9.	CAVE	I. Tom's notepaper
V - 10.	HUCK	J. Place where Tom and Becky got lost
O - 11.	POLLY	K. The boys attended their own
E - 12.	WIG	L. The cat
N - 13.	TREASURE	M. Tom gave some to Peter, making him act crazy: ___ killer
Q - 14.	CUFFS	N. You have to dig for it where the shadow of a dead tree limb falls at midnight.
R - 15.	SKIFF	O. Tom's guardian
W - 16.	SMOKE	P. He took the blame for tearing the teacher's book.
A - 17.	GANG	Q. Tom got these and kisses from Aunt Polly upon his return.
I - 18.	BARK	R. Small boat
H - 19.	COURT	S. Tom could do this through the gap in his teeth.
B - 20.	PIRATES	T. Tom blew out Becky's to conserve.
F - 21.	WELSHMAN	U. Tom's half-brother
T - 22.	CANDLE	V. Son of the town drunk
S - 23.	SPIT	W. Huck taught Tom & Joe how to do this bad habit.
L - 24.	PETER	X. Doctor Injun Joe killed
Y - 25.	FINN	Y. Huck's last name

Copyrighted

Tom Sawyer Matching 4

___ 1. CANDLE   A. Author
___ 2. PAIN   B. Tom got these and kisses from Aunt Polly upon his return.
___ 3. CAVE   C. Tom's name was printed in it for telling on Injun Joe
___ 4. DOUGLAS   D. Sunday school superintendent
___ 5. WITNESS   E. A gory one was found next to Dr. Robinson
___ 6. MARY   F. Food for island boys
___ 7. CATS   G. The teacher
___ 8. DOBBINS   H. Group of boys; Tom Sawyer's ___
___ 9. MURDER   I. Tom's girl cousin
___10. POTTER   J. Tom was one to Dr. Robinson's murder.
___11. SID   K. Place where Tom and Becky got lost
___12. NEWSPAPER   L. The widow
___13. KNIFE   M. Muff; drunk accused of murder
___14. POLLY   N. Tom gave some to Peter, making him act crazy: ___ killer
___15. TOM   O. Tom blew out Becky's to conserve.
___16. JACKSON   P. Small boat
___17. SKIFF   Q. ____'s Island
___18. WALTERS   R. What Tom and Huck witnessed in the graveyard
___19. GANG   S. He took the blame for tearing the teacher's book.
___20. FENCE   T. You have to dig for it where the shadow of a dead tree limb falls at midnight.
___21. TWAIN   U. Tom's half-brother
___22. FISH   V. Tom was supposed to whitewash it
___23. TREASURE   W. Dead ones are good for curing warts.
___24. CUFFS   X. Tom's guardian
___25. WIG   Y. The boys stole Mr. Dobbins's

Tom Sawyer Matching 4 Answer Key

O - 1.	CANDLE	A. Author
N - 2.	PAIN	B. Tom got these and kisses from Aunt Polly upon his return.
K - 3.	CAVE	C. Tom's name was printed in it for telling on Injun Joe
L - 4.	DOUGLAS	D. Sunday school superintendent
J - 5.	WITNESS	E. A gory one was found next to Dr. Robinson
I - 6.	MARY	F. Food for island boys
W - 7.	CATS	G. The teacher
G - 8.	DOBBINS	H. Group of boys; Tom Sawyer's ___
R - 9.	MURDER	I. Tom's girl cousin
M - 10.	POTTER	J. Tom was one to Dr. Robinson's murder.
U - 11.	SID	K. Place where Tom and Becky got lost
C - 12.	NEWSPAPER	L. The widow
E - 13.	KNIFE	M. Muff; drunk accused of murder
X - 14.	POLLY	N. Tom gave some to Peter, making him act crazy: ___ killer
S - 15.	TOM	O. Tom blew out Becky's to conserve.
Q - 16.	JACKSON	P. Small boat
P - 17.	SKIFF	Q. ____'s Island
D - 18.	WALTERS	R. What Tom and Huck witnessed in the graveyard
H - 19.	GANG	S. He took the blame for tearing the teacher's book.
V - 20.	FENCE	T. You have to dig for it where the shadow of a dead tree limb falls at midnight.
A - 21.	TWAIN	U. Tom's half-brother
F - 22.	FISH	V. Tom was supposed to whitewash it
T - 23.	TREASURE	W. Dead ones are good for curing warts.
B - 24.	CUFFS	X. Tom's guardian
Y - 25.	WIG	Y. The boys stole Mr. Dobbins's

Tom Sawyer Magic Squares 1

Match the definition with the vocabulary word. Put your answers in the magic squares below. When your answers are correct, all columns and rows will add to the same number.

A. CAVE	E. MURDER	I. KNIFE	M. POTTER
B. WIG	F. CANDLE	J. SAWYER	N. TOM
C. SKIFF	G. FINN	K. PINCHBUG	O. DOUGLAS
D. JOE	H. TREASURE	L. PETER	P. CUFFS

1. Muff; drunk accused of murder
2. Tom blew out Becky's to conserve.
3. You have to dig for it where the shadow of a dead tree limb falls at midnight.
4. The widow
5. The cat
6. Small boat
7. Place where Tom and Becky got lost
8. Tom's last name
9. Tom passed time in church by watching this.
10. Went to island with Huck and Tom
11. The boys stole Mr. Dobbins's
12. A gory one was found next to Dr. Robinson
13. He took the blame for tearing the teacher's book.
14. What Tom and Huck witnessed in the graveyard
15. Huck's last name
16. Tom got these and kisses from Aunt Polly upon his return.

A=	B=	C=	D=
E=	F=	G=	H=
I=	J=	K=	L=
M=	N=	O=	P=

Tom Sawyer Magic Squares 1 Answer Key

Match the definition with the vocabulary word. Put your answers in the magic squares below. When your answers are correct, all columns and rows will add to the same number.

A. CAVE	E. MURDER	I. KNIFE	M. POTTER
B. WIG	F. CANDLE	J. SAWYER	N. TOM
C. SKIFF	G. FINN	K. PINCHBUG	O. DOUGLAS
D. JOE	H. TREASURE	L. PETER	P. CUFFS

1. Muff; drunk accused of murder
2. Tom blew out Becky's to conserve.
3. You have to dig for it where the shadow of a dead tree limb falls at midnight.
4. The widow
5. The cat
6. Small boat
7. Place where Tom and Becky got lost
8. Tom's last name
9. Tom passed time in church by watching this.
10. Went to island with Huck and Tom
11. The boys stole Mr. Dobbins's
12. A gory one was found next to Dr. Robinson
13. He took the blame for tearing the teacher's book.
14. What Tom and Huck witnessed in the graveyard
15. Huck's last name
16. Tom got these and kisses from Aunt Polly upon his return.

A=7	B=11	C=6	D=10
E=14	F=2	G=15	H=3
I=12	J=8	K=9	L=5
M=1	N=13	O=4	P=16

Tom Sawyer Magic Squares 2

Match the definition with the vocabulary word. Put your answers in the magic squares below. When your answers are correct, all columns and rows will add to the same number.

A. ROBINSON   E. BARK   I. INJUN   M. CAVE
B. PETER   F. FENCE   J. SPADE   N. MARY
C. MISSISSIPPI G. POLLY   K. TREASURE   O. TOM
D. THATCHER   H. KNIFE   L. WIG   P. PIRATES

1. A gory one was found next to Dr. Robinson
2. Place where Tom and Becky got lost
3. The cat
4. You have to dig for it where the shadow of a dead tree limb falls at midnight.
5. The boys left it and the pick downstairs.
6. The river
7. They wore fancy clothes.
8. Tom's notepaper
9. He took the blame for tearing the teacher's book.
10. Tom was supposed to whitewash it
11. Murderer: ___ Joe
12. Becky's last name
13. Doctor Injun Joe killed
14. The boys stole Mr. Dobbins's
15. Tom's guardian
16. Tom's girl cousin

A=	B=	C=	D=
E=	F=	G=	H=
I=	J=	K=	L=
M=	N=	O=	P=

Tom Sawyer Magic Squares 2 Answer Key

Match the definition with the vocabulary word. Put your answers in the magic squares below. When your answers are correct, all columns and rows will add to the same number.

A. ROBINSON E. BARK   I. INJUN   M. CAVE
B. PETER   F. FENCE J. SPADE   N. MARY
C. MISSISSIPPI G. POLLY K. TREASURE O. TOM
D. THATCHER H. KNIFE L. WIG   P. PIRATES

1. A gory one was found next to Dr. Robinson
2. Place where Tom and Becky got lost
3. The cat
4. You have to dig for it where the shadow of a dead tree limb falls at midnight.
5. The boys left it and the pick downstairs.
6. The river
7. They wore fancy clothes.
8. Tom's notepaper
9. He took the blame for tearing the teacher's book.
10. Tom was supposed to whitewash it
11. Murderer: ___ Joe
12. Becky's last name
13. Doctor Injun Joe killed
14. The boys stole Mr. Dobbins's
15. Tom's guardian
16. Tom's girl cousin

A=13	B=3	C=6	D=12
E=8	F=10	G=15	H=1
I=11	J=5	K=4	L=14
M=2	N=16	O=9	P=7

Tom Sawyer Magic Squares 3

Match the definition with the vocabulary word. Put your answers in the magic squares below. When your answers are correct, all columns and rows will add to the same number.

A. PETERSBURG E. BARK   I. WITCHES   M. THATCHER
B. TOE   F. SPIT   J. CONSCIENCE N. INJUN
C. JOE   G. TWAIN K. FUNERAL   O. SMOKE
D. PETER   H. AMY   L. GANG   P. TWO

1. Tom could do this through the gap in his teeth.
2. Tom blamed the unsuccessful marble spell on these.
3. Huck taught Tom & Joe how to do this bad habit.
4. The cat
5. Becky's last name
6. Tom had a sore one.
7. Tom had been engaged to her before Becky.
8. The boys attended their own
9. Went to island with Huck and Tom
10. Number __
11. Tom brought things to Muff Potter to ease his ___.
12. Tom's notepaper
13. Group of boys; Tom Sawyer's ___
14. Author
15. Tom's town: St. ___
16. Murderer: ___ Joe

A=	B=	C=	D=
E=	F=	G=	H=
I=	J=	K=	L=
M=	N=	O=	P=

Tom Sawyer Magic Squares 3 Answer Key

Match the definition with the vocabulary word. Put your answers in the magic squares below. When your answers are correct, all columns and rows will add to the same number.

A. PETERSBURG   E. BARK   I. WITCHES   M. THATCHER
B. TOE   F. SPIT   J. CONSCIENCE   N. INJUN
C. JOE   G. TWAIN   K. FUNERAL   O. SMOKE
D. PETER   H. AMY   L. GANG   P. TWO

1. Tom could do this through the gap in his teeth.
2. Tom blamed the unsuccessful marble spell on these.
3. Huck taught Tom & Joe how to do this bad habit.
4. The cat
5. Becky's last name
6. Tom had a sore one.
7. Tom had been engaged to her before Becky.
8. The boys attended their own
9. Went to island with Huck and Tom
10. Number __
11. Tom brought things to Muff Potter to ease his ___.
12. Tom's notepaper
13. Group of boys; Tom Sawyer's ___
14. Author
15. Tom's town: St. ___
16. Murderer: ___ Joe

A=15	B=6	C=9	D=4
E=12	F=1	G=14	H=7
I=2	J=11	K=8	L=13
M=5	N=16	O=3	P=10

Tom Sawyer Magic Squares 4

Match the definition with the vocabulary word. Put your answers in the magic squares below. When your answers are correct, all columns and rows will add to the same number.

A. SPADE
B. INK
C. TRAPPED
D. MISSISSIPPI
E. PINCHBUG
F. JACKSON
G. COURT
H. FISH
I. GANG
J. CUFFS
K. POLLY
L. TWAIN
M. TICKETS
N. FENCE
O. BECKY
P. FINN

1. It spilled on Tom's spelling book.
2. Place where the trial is held
3. Tom's guardian
4. Tom was supposed to whitewash it
5. Ten yellow ones were redeemed for a Bible.
6. Author
7. Food for island boys
8. The boys left it and the pick downstairs.
9. Huck's last name
10. Group of boys; Tom Sawyer's ___
11. Tom passed time in church by watching this.
12. The river
13. Injun Joe got ___ in the cave and died.
14. ___'s Island
15. Tom got these and kisses from Aunt Polly upon his return.
16. She was engaged to Tom.

A=	B=	C=	D=
E=	F=	G=	H=
I=	J=	K=	L=
M=	N=	O=	P=

Tom Sawyer Magic Squares 4 Answer Key

Match the definition with the vocabulary word. Put your answers in the magic squares below. When your answers are correct, all columns and rows will add to the same number.

A. SPADE   E. PINCHBUG   I. GANG   M. TICKETS
B. INK   F. JACKSON   J. CUFFS   N. FENCE
C. TRAPPED   G. COURT   K. POLLY   O. BECKY
D. MISSISSIPPI   H. FISH   L. TWAIN   P. FINN

1. It spilled on Tom's spelling book.
2. Place where the trial is held
3. Tom's guardian
4. Tom was supposed to whitewash it
5. Ten yellow ones were redeemed for a Bible.
6. Author
7. Food for island boys
8. The boys left it and the pick downstairs.
9. Huck's last name
10. Group of boys; Tom Sawyer's ___
11. Tom passed time in church by watching this.
12. The river
13. Injun Joe got ___ in the cave and died.
14. ____'s Island
15. Tom got these and kisses from Aunt Polly upon his return.
16. She was engaged to Tom.

A=8	B=1	C=13	D=12
E=11	F=14	G=2	H=7
I=10	J=15	K=3	L=6
M=5	N=4	O=16	P=9

Tom Sawyer Word Search 1

```
C H M W Z T H T I C K E T S D K L P N
V O C G Y O D P S T F P K L P N F N K
T Q N H U M I S S I S S I P P I I Z X
M A H S U D R V E K Q H Y R S F T W Y
G L E R C B N Y N D I P K H A N L D V
L R D C I I K C T B O F J T V T R D V
F E N C E N E D I S C U F F S H E O T
R T L L I A J N W G A V G N B R H S D
P T L F G M G U C Z S W E L F P C H L
C O E K L H P S N E R M Y L A Y T B B
L P Q Q E S M O K E E B A E L S A C V
L S H D G L H M R L T Y O L R R H O T
T R A P P E D U C Q L J O X K Y T U K
R P M Y C W S Z T W A P Y M K C R R Y
S W R T W A I N B W W H U C K C A T S
H A Z I E M K I O N O V E T B K D V J
M S G R Z Y X A O Y Y B L P E T E R E
W I T C H E S P K C A N D L E M D V B
```

A gory one was found next to Dr. Robinson (5)
AKA Twain (7)
Author (5)
Becky tore the teacher's (4)
Becky's last name (8)
Dead ones are good for curing warts. (4)
Food for island boys (4)
Group of boys; Tom Sawyer's ___ (4)
Haunted ___ (5)
He saved Widow Douglas. (8)
He took the blame for tearing the teacher's book. (3)
How Tom got his tickets (6)
Huck taught Tom & Joe how to do this bad habit. (5)
Huck's last name (4)
Injun Joe got ___ in the cave and died. (7)
It spilled on Tom's spelling book. (3)
Muff; drunk accused of murder (6)
Murderer: ___ Joe (5)
New boy; spilled ink on Tom's book (6)
Number __ (3)
Place where Tom and Becky got lost (4)
Place where the trial is held (5)
She was engaged to Tom. (5)
Small boat (5)
Son of the town drunk (4)
Sunday school superintendent (7)
Ten yellow ones were redeemed for a Bible. (7)
The boys left it and the pick downstairs. (5)

The boys stole Mr. Dobbins's (3)
The cat (5)
The river (11)
The widow (7)
They wore fancy clothes. (7)
Tom blamed the unsuccessful marble spell on these. (7)
Tom blew out Becky's to conserve. (6)
Tom brought things to Muff Potter to ease his ___. (10)
Tom could do this through the gap in his teeth. (4)
Tom gave some to Peter, making him act crazy: ___ killer (4)
Tom got these and kisses from Aunt Polly upon his return. (5)
Tom had a sore one. (3)
Tom had been engaged to her before Becky. (3)
Tom was one to Dr. Robinson's murder. (7)
Tom was supposed to whitewash it (5)
Tom's girl cousin (4)
Tom's guardian (5)
Tom's half-brother (3)
Tom's last name (6)
Tom's notepaper (4)
Went to island with Huck and Tom (3)
What Tom and Huck witnessed in the graveyard (6)
You have to dig for it where the shadow of a dead tree limb falls at midnight. (8)

Tom Sawyer Word Search 1 Answer Key

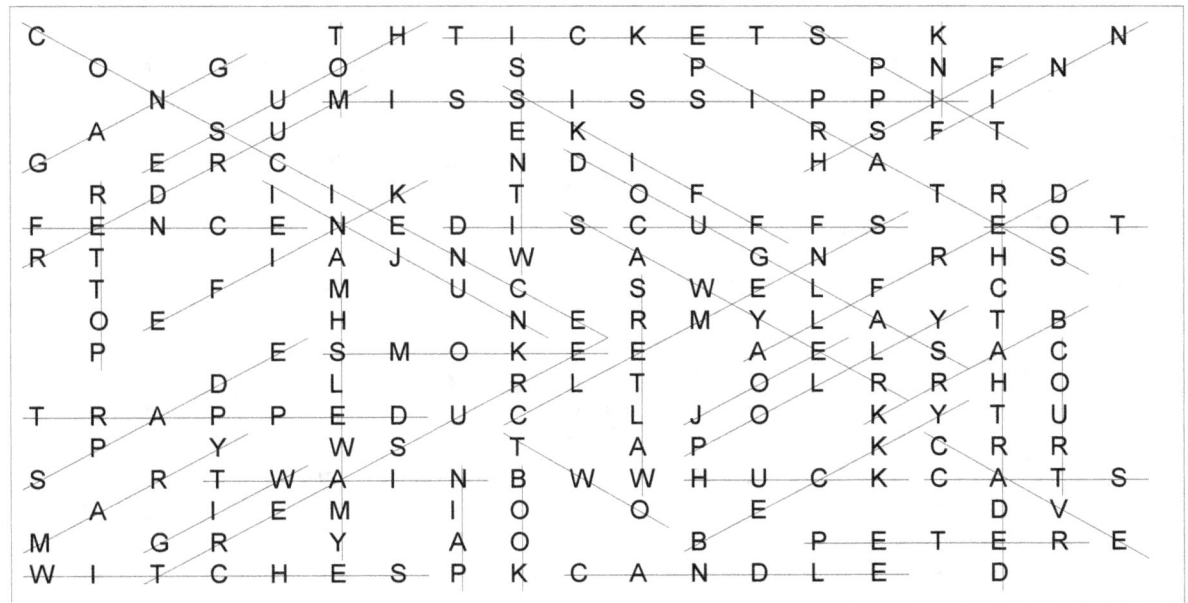

A gory one was found next to Dr. Robinson (5)
AKA Twain (7)
Author (5)
Becky tore the teacher's (4)
Becky's last name (8)
Dead ones are good for curing warts. (4)
Food for island boys (4)
Group of boys; Tom Sawyer's ___ (4)
Haunted ___ (5)
He saved Widow Douglas. (8)
He took the blame for tearing the teacher's book. (3)
How Tom got his tickets (6)
Huck taught Tom & Joe how to do this bad habit. (5)
Huck's last name (4)
Injun Joe got ___ in the cave and died. (7)
It spilled on Tom's spelling book. (3)
Muff; drunk accused of murder (6)
Murderer: ___ Joe (5)
New boy; spilled ink on Tom's book (6)
Number __ (3)
Place where Tom and Becky got lost (4)
Place where the trial is held (5)
She was engaged to Tom. (5)
Small boat (5)
Son of the town drunk (4)
Sunday school superintendent (7)
Ten yellow ones were redeemed for a Bible. (7)
The boys left it and the pick downstairs. (5)

The boys stole Mr. Dobbins's (3)
The cat (5)
The river (11)
The widow (7)
They wore fancy clothes. (7)
Tom blamed the unsuccessful marble spell on these. (7)
Tom blew out Becky's to conserve. (6)
Tom brought things to Muff Potter to ease his ___. (10)
Tom could do this through the gap in his teeth. (4)
Tom gave some to Peter, making him act crazy: ___ killer (4)
Tom got these and kisses from Aunt Polly upon his return. (5)
Tom had a sore one. (3)
Tom had been engaged to her before Becky. (3)
Tom was one to Dr. Robinson's murder. (7)
Tom was supposed to whitewash it (5)
Tom's girl cousin (4)
Tom's guardian (5)
Tom's half-brother (3)
Tom's last name (6)
Tom's notepaper (4)
Went to island with Huck and Tom (3)
What Tom and Huck witnessed in the graveyard (6)
You have to dig for it where the shadow of a dead tree limb falls at midnight. (8)

Tom Sawyer Word Search 2

```
E L D N A C W Y J D P W I T C H E S M
C W K H Q G K I H O O O B X L U W V C
N A P R B C P Y G B T T L Z R B F O N
E L S J E P K J S B T D C L G A U F O
I T H B T S I H Z I E W A N Y R C Q S
C E X L F L I R K N R Q A L T K K B N
S R W E P A D N A S W W K I F C T M I
N S V I L R Y Q J T T H S D N R G U B
O A R A T E S N R U E R T J S T E R O
C L E M E N S P A I N S A L G U O D R
C Q H Y N U E N M Z G C C D M A E E P
S T G I N F E S P B K Z X B E P N R P
Q I F C E S M G S S F I S H P D J G P
M C D C U M A J O P F F F A H Y S O R
Y K N O W O R N S A I Z R U W R D E E
P E H W D K Y P J D K T C Y H Y T R M
F T T W O E I N K E S K N I F E E O X
Y S T H A T C H E R B O O K P X T R W
```

A gory one was found next to Dr. Robinson (5)
AKA Twain (7)
Author (5)
Becky tore the teacher's (4)
Becky's last name (8)
Dead ones are good for curing warts. (4)
Doctor Injun Joe killed (8)
Food for island boys (4)
Group of boys; Tom Sawyer's ___ (4)
Haunted ___ (5)
He took the blame for tearing the teacher's book. (3)
How Tom got his tickets (6)
Huck taught Tom & Joe how to do this bad habit. (5)
Huck's last name (4)
Injun Joe got ___ in the cave and died. (7)
It spilled on Tom's spelling book. (3)
Muff; drunk accused of murder (6)
Murderer: ___ Joe (5)
New boy; spilled ink on Tom's book (6)
Number __ (3)
Place where Tom and Becky got lost (4)
Place where the trial is held (5)
She was engaged to Tom. (5)
Small boat (5)
Son of the town drunk (4)
Sunday school superintendent (7)
Ten yellow ones were redeemed for a Bible. (7)
The boys attended their own (7)

The boys left it and the pick downstairs. (5)
The boys stole Mr. Dobbins's (3)
The cat (5)
The teacher (7)
The widow (7)
They wore fancy clothes. (7)
Tom blamed the unsuccessful marble spell on these. (7)
Tom blew out Becky's to conserve. (6)
Tom brought things to Muff Potter to ease his ___. (10)
Tom could do this through the gap in his teeth. (4)
Tom gave some to Peter, making him act crazy: ___ killer (4)
Tom got these and kisses from Aunt Polly upon his return. (5)
Tom had a sore one. (3)
Tom had been engaged to her before Becky. (3)
Tom was one to Dr. Robinson's murder. (7)
Tom was supposed to whitewash it (5)
Tom's girl cousin (4)
Tom's guardian (5)
Tom's half-brother (3)
Tom's last name (6)
Tom's notepaper (4)
Went to island with Huck and Tom (3)
What Tom and Huck witnessed in the graveyard (6)
____'s Island (7)

Tom Sawyer Word Search 2 Answer Key

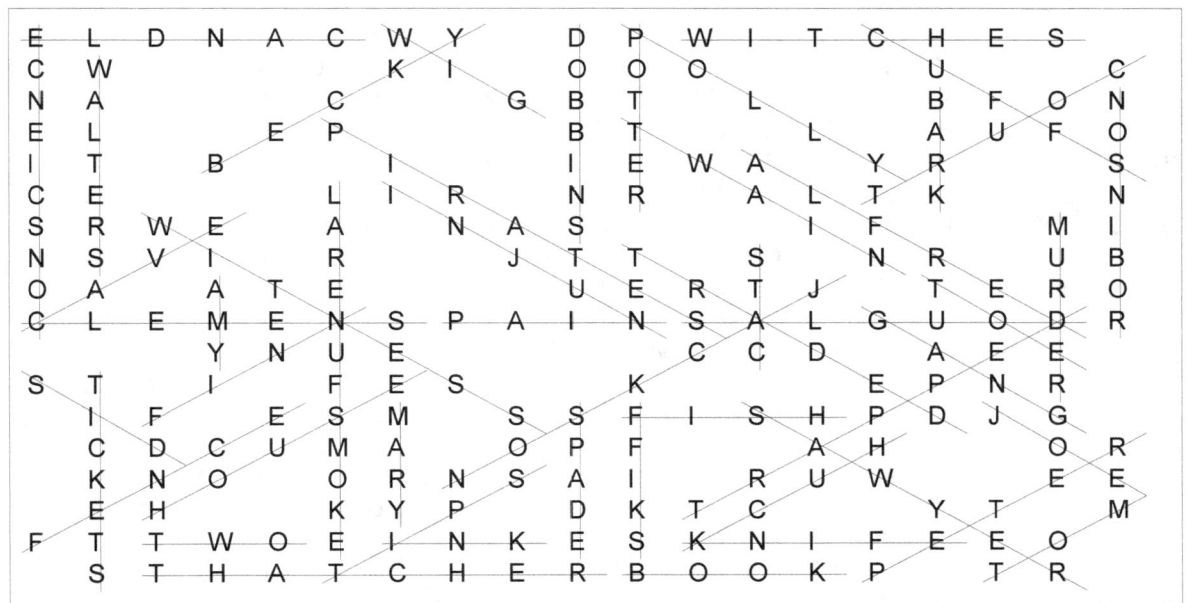

A gory one was found next to Dr. Robinson (5)
AKA Twain (7)
Author (5)
Becky tore the teacher's (4)
Becky's last name (8)
Dead ones are good for curing warts. (4)
Doctor Injun Joe killed (8)
Food for island boys (4)
Group of boys; Tom Sawyer's ___ (4)
Haunted ___ (5)
He took the blame for tearing the teacher's book. (3)
How Tom got his tickets (6)
Huck taught Tom & Joe how to do this bad habit. (5)
Huck's last name (4)
Injun Joe got ___ in the cave and died. (7)
It spilled on Tom's spelling book. (3)
Muff; drunk accused of murder (6)
Murderer: ___ Joe (5)
New boy; spilled ink on Tom's book (6)
Number __ (3)
Place where Tom and Becky got lost (4)
Place where the trial is held (5)
She was engaged to Tom. (5)
Small boat (5)
Son of the town drunk (4)
Sunday school superintendent (7)
Ten yellow ones were redeemed for a Bible. (7)
The boys attended their own (7)

The boys left it and the pick downstairs. (5)
The boys stole Mr. Dobbins's (3)
The cat (5)
The teacher (7)
The widow (7)
They wore fancy clothes. (7)
Tom blamed the unsuccessful marble spell on these. (7)
Tom blew out Becky's to conserve. (6)
Tom brought things to Muff Potter to ease his ___. (10)
Tom could do this through the gap in his teeth. (4)
Tom gave some to Peter, making him act crazy: ___ killer (4)
Tom got these and kisses from Aunt Polly upon his return. (5)
Tom had a sore one. (3)
Tom had been engaged to her before Becky. (3)
Tom was one to Dr. Robinson's murder. (7)
Tom was supposed to whitewash it (5)
Tom's girl cousin (4)
Tom's guardian (5)
Tom's half-brother (3)
Tom's last name (6)
Tom's notepaper (4)
Went to island with Huck and Tom (3)
What Tom and Huck witnessed in the graveyard (6)
____'s Island (7)

Tom Sawyer Word Search 3

```
R Z X S A L G U O D S X D Y T R L W Q Z
O C I N K Y P E T E R S B U R G W I G G
B K Q O M I O L T L M C K E A U B T K F
I Q O A F J F A J O Z C T B P B W C N D
N B X S P U R F K H K T H J P H B H I L
S P I T X I N E F C O U R T E C N E F C
O V O A P N A E K P C U R C D N T S E H
N E A C W J M N R K N M S Z A I R P L T
K M N L J U H B X A T X G E P P E C Y J
P A I N F N S R E T L A W Z S P A P E T
V R H V G R L L O W I Y H B H N S E C N
V Y L M A P E M N O N C F F D N U T N L
G T G E N H W D V M E S K L P I R E E T
Z D V F G I Y H S S W E E J F E R I T T
K A J R T K M L N F S B S Q T R Z L C H
C X K N C N V E I F P A A G G S N D S W
T C E E D K M S B U A R W Q B P B S N K
P S B K R E F I B C P K Y J A C K S O N
S B S T L V I D O C E R E D R U M V C H
G G Q C W J S W D S R T R A D E D G H S
P O L L Y T H A T C H E R T W A I N W H
```

ALFRED	DOBBINS	JOE	ROBINSON	TRAPPED
AMY	DOUGLAS	KNIFE	SAWYER	TREASURE
BARK	FENCE	MARY	SID	TWAIN
BECKY	FINN	MURDER	SKIFF	TWO
BOOK	FISH	NEWSPAPER	SMOKE	WALTERS
CANDLE	FUNERAL	PAIN	SPADE	WELSHMAN
CATS	GANG	PETER	SPIT	WIG
CAVE	HOUSE	PETERSBURG	THATCHER	WITCHES
CLEMENS	HUCK	PINCHBUG	TICKETS	WITNESS
CONSCIENCE	INJUN	PIRATES	TOE	
COURT	INK	POLLY	TOM	
CUFFS	JACKSON	POTTER	TRADED	

Tom Sawyer Word Search 3 Answer Key

ALFRED	DOBBINS	JOE	ROBINSON	TRAPPED
AMY	DOUGLAS	KNIFE	SAWYER	TREASURE
BARK	FENCE	MARY	SID	TWAIN
BECKY	FINN	MURDER	SKIFF	TWO
BOOK	FISH	NEWSPAPER	SMOKE	WALTERS
CANDLE	FUNERAL	PAIN	SPADE	WELSHMAN
CATS	GANG	PETER	SPIT	WIG
CAVE	HOUSE	PETERSBURG	THATCHER	WITCHES
CLEMENS	HUCK	PINCHBUG	TICKETS	WITNESS
CONSCIENCE	INJUN	PIRATES	TOE	
COURT	INK	POLLY	TOM	
CUFFS	JACKSON	POTTER	TRADED	

Tom Sawyer Word Search 4

```
W C R E P A P S W E N P D T V S B K Z B
I A F L T A T Z J G F F O F W Q M J N P
G V L J G F I I A X U P J T I B K O H F
W E L S H M A N U J N I A W T H A E K R
Z S G T P W G K F Q E R D O C E W R D E
Z Q W E F I I F P J R A E N H G R B K G
L R G K I Q T T B R A T R S E H K T M T
W F Z C N R C Y N P L E N O S N I B O R
P A Q I N D L O N E R S P I I P N N R M
E D L T Q L R O U X S N F F D B A E B J
T O Y T O Y S W X R J S E Y H J Y D R B
E B R P E K M A R Y T S C M T W O T E G
R B W S C R V V K P M U L A A G B R D S
S I V A N H S C L S F Q E S N D R A R L
B N J N R P E P A F K V M C T D T P U D
U S W E T B M L S L G F E N L R L P M G
R P T W Q H G Z B S F P N Z A F H E H G
G E T S R U M R O K M R S D Z E O D G W
P F Y Y O C G N O I J S E Z S N U G L M
Y V K D M K D D K F W D M D Q C S C R X
T R E A S U R E S F C A T S D E E D N Z
```

ALFRED	DOBBINS	JACKSON	POTTER	TRADED
AMY	DOUGLAS	JOE	ROBINSON	TRAPPED
BARK	FENCE	KNIFE	SAWYER	TREASURE
BECKY	FINN	MARY	SID	TWAIN
BOOK	FISH	MURDER	SKIFF	TWO
CANDLE	FUNERAL	NEWSPAPER	SMOKE	WALTERS
CATS	GANG	PAIN	SPADE	WELSHMAN
CAVE	HOUSE	PETER	SPIT	WIG
CLEMENS	HUCK	PETERSBURG	TICKETS	WITCHES
COURT	INJUN	PIRATES	TOE	WITNESS
CUFFS	INK	POLLY	TOM	

Tom Sawyer Word Search 4 Answer Key

ALFRED	DOBBINS	JACKSON	POTTER	TRADED
AMY	DOUGLAS	JOE	ROBINSON	TRAPPED
BARK	FENCE	KNIFE	SAWYER	TREASURE
BECKY	FINN	MARY	SID	TWAIN
BOOK	FISH	MURDER	SKIFF	TWO
CANDLE	FUNERAL	NEWSPAPER	SMOKE	WALTERS
CATS	GANG	PAIN	SPADE	WELSHMAN
CAVE	HOUSE	PETER	SPIT	WIG
CLEMENS	HUCK	PETERSBURG	TICKETS	WITCHES
COURT	INJUN	PIRATES	TOE	WITNESS
CUFFS	INK	POLLY	TOM	

Tom Sawyer Crossword 1

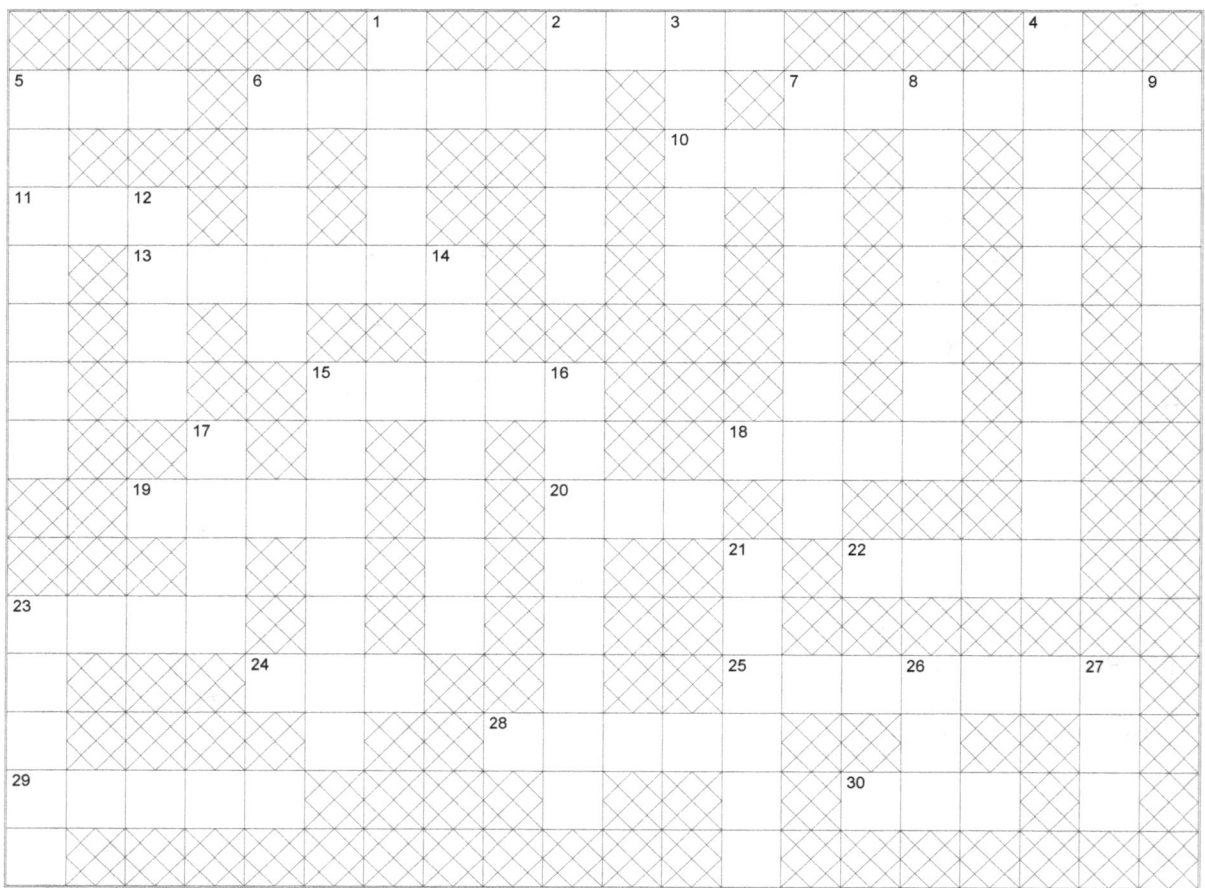

Across
2. Tom gave some to Peter, making him act crazy: ___ killer
5. The boys stole Mr. Dobbins's
6. Tom blew out Becky's to conserve.
7. Tom was one to Dr. Robinson's murder.
10. Went to island with Huck and Tom
11. He took the blame for tearing the teacher's book.
13. New boy; spilled ink on Tom's book
15. Place where the trial is held
18. Dead ones are good for curing warts.
19. Place where Tom and Becky got lost
20. Tom had been engaged to her before Becky.
22. Group of boys; Tom Sawyer's ___
23. Son of the town drunk
24. It spilled on Tom's spelling book.
25. Sunday school superintendent
28. She was engaged to Tom.
29. The boys left it and the pick downstairs.
30. Tom had a sore one.

Down
1. A gory one was found next to Dr. Robinson
2. The cat
3. Murderer: ___ Joe
4. Tom's town: St. ___
5. Tom blamed the unsuccessful marble spell on these.
6. Tom got these and kisses from Aunt Polly upon his return.
7. He saved Widow Douglas.
8. Ten yellow ones were redeemed for a Bible.
9. Small boat
12. Tom's girl cousin
14. The widow
15. AKA Twain
16. Becky's last name
17. Tom's notepaper
21. Tom's last name
23. Haunted ___
26. Number ___
27. Tom's half-brother

Tom Sawyer Crossword 1 Answer Key

				¹K		²P	A	³I	N			⁴P	
⁵W	I	G		⁶C	A	N	D	L	E		⁷W	⁸I	T	N	E	S	⁹S
I				U		I		T		¹⁰J	O	E		I		T		K
¹¹T	¹²O	M		F		F		E		U		L		C		E		I
C	¹³A	L	F	R	E	¹⁴D		R		N		S		K		R		F
H	R		S			O						H		E		S		F
E	Y			¹⁵C	O	U	R	¹⁶T				M		T		B		
S		¹⁷B		L		G		H			¹⁸C	A	T	S		U		
	¹⁹C	A	V	E		L		²⁰A	M	Y		N				R		
		R		M		A		T			²¹S	²²G	A	N	G			
²³H	U	C	K	E		S		C			A							
O			²⁴I	N	K			H			²⁵W		²⁶T		²⁷S		
U				S			²⁸B	E	C	K	Y		W		I		
²⁹S	P	A	D	E			R				E		³⁰T	O	E		D
E							R				R						

Across

2. Tom gave some to Peter, making him act crazy: ___ killer
5. The boys stole Mr. Dobbins's
6. Tom blew out Becky's to conserve.
7. Tom was one to Dr. Robinson's murder.
10. Went to island with Huck and Tom
11. He took the blame for tearing the teacher's book.
13. New boy; spilled ink on Tom's book
15. Place where the trial is held
18. Dead ones are good for curing warts.
19. Place where Tom and Becky got lost
20. Tom had been engaged to her before Becky.
22. Group of boys; Tom Sawyer's ___
23. Son of the town drunk
24. It spilled on Tom's spelling book.
25. Sunday school superintendent
28. She was engaged to Tom.
29. The boys left it and the pick downstairs.
30. Tom had a sore one.

Down

1. A gory one was found next to Dr. Robinson
2. The cat
3. Murderer: ___ Joe
4. Tom's town: St. ___
5. Tom blamed the unsuccessful marble spell on these.
6. Tom got these and kisses from Aunt Polly upon his return.
7. He saved Widow Douglas.
8. Ten yellow ones were redeemed for a Bible.
9. Small boat
12. Tom's girl cousin
14. The widow
15. AKA Twain
16. Becky's last name
17. Tom's notepaper
21. Tom's last name
23. Haunted ___
26. Number __
27. Tom's half-brother

Tom Sawyer Crossword 2

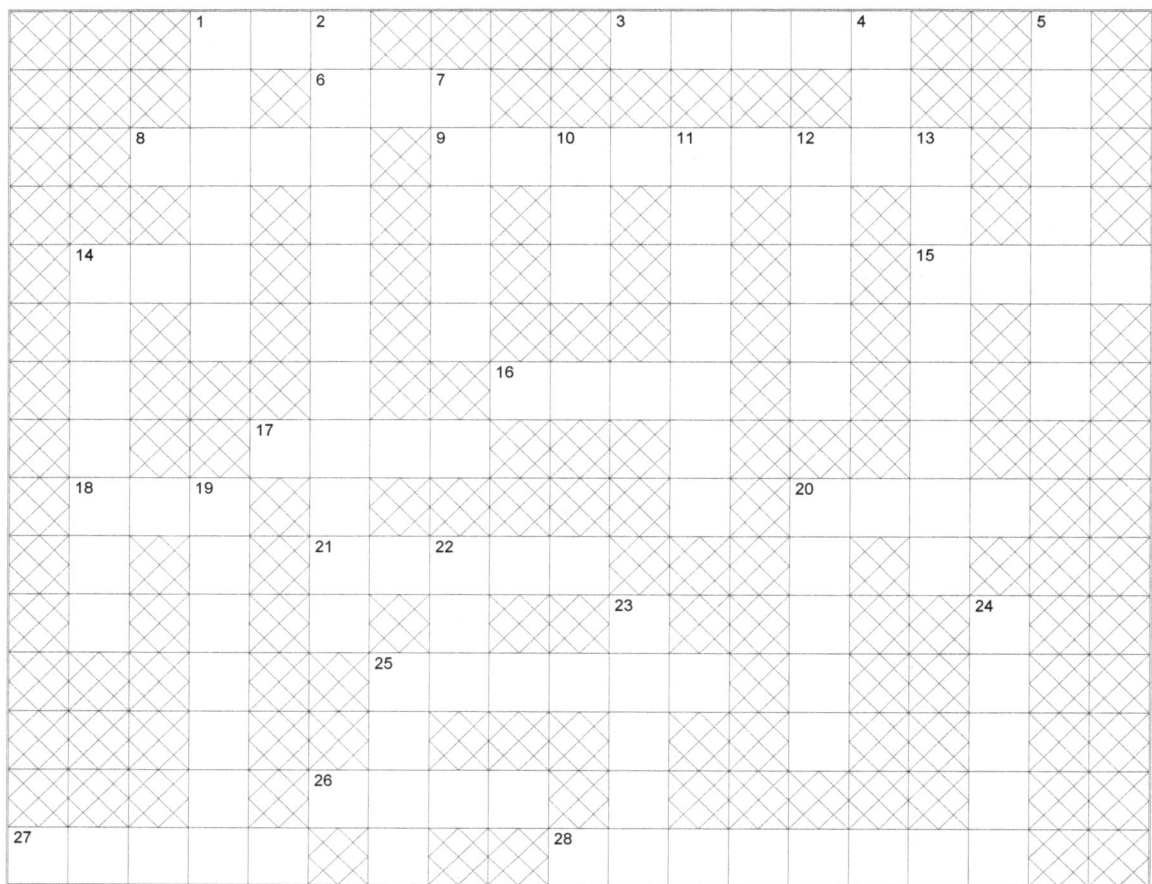

Across
1. He took the blame for tearing the teacher's book.
3. Place where the trial is held
6. It spilled on Tom's spelling book.
8. Dead ones are good for curing warts.
9. Tom's name was printed in it for telling on Injun Joe
14. Went to island with Huck and Tom
15. Tom's notepaper
16. Tom could do this through the gap in his teeth.
17. Huck's last name
18. Tom's half-brother
20. Becky tore the teacher's
21. The cat
25. Muff; drunk accused of murder
26. Food for island boys
27. Haunted ___
28. He saved Widow Douglas.

Down
1. How Tom got his tickets
2. The river
4. Tom had a sore one.
5. The boys attended their own
7. A gory one was found next to Dr. Robinson
10. The boys stole Mr. Dobbins's
11. They wore fancy clothes.
12. Tom's guardian
13. Doctor Injun Joe killed
14. ___'s Island
19. The widow
20. She was engaged to Tom.
22. Number ___
23. Tom was supposed to whitewash it
24. Murderer: ___ Joe
25. Tom gave some to Peter, making him act crazy: ___ killer

Tom Sawyer Crossword 2 Answer Key

		1 T	O	2 M			3 C	O	U	R	4 T		5 F	
		R		6 I	7 N	K					O		U	
	8 C	A	T	S		9 N	10 E	11 W	S	12 P	A	13 P	E	R	N
		D		S		I		I		I		O		O		E
	14 J	O	E		I		F		G		R		L		15 B	A	R	K
	A		D		S		E				A		L		I		A	
	C			S		16 S	P	I	T		Y		N		L	
	K		17 F	I	N	N				E			S		
18 S	I	19 D	E					20 B	O	O	K		
	O		O		21 P	22 E	T	E	R			E		N	
	N		U		I		W		23 F			C		24 I
		G		25 P	O	T	T	E	R		K		N	
		L		A				N		Y		J	
		A	26 F	I	S	H		C				U	
27 H	O	U	S	E		N		28 W	E	L	S	H	M	A	N

Across
1. He took the blame for tearing the teacher's book.
3. Place where the trial is held
6. It spilled on Tom's spelling book.
8. Dead ones are good for curing warts.
9. Tom's name was printed in it for telling on Injun Joe
14. Went to island with Huck and Tom
15. Tom's notepaper
16. Tom could do this through the gap in his teeth.
17. Huck's last name
18. Tom's half-brother
20. Becky tore the teacher's
21. The cat
25. Muff; drunk accused of murder
26. Food for island boys
27. Haunted ___
28. He saved Widow Douglas.

Down
1. How Tom got his tickets
2. The river
4. Tom had a sore one.
5. The boys attended their own
7. A gory one was found next to Dr. Robinson
10. The boys stole Mr. Dobbins's
11. They wore fancy clothes.
12. Tom's guardian
13. Doctor Injun Joe killed
14. ___'s Island
19. The widow
20. She was engaged to Tom.
22. Number ___
23. Tom was supposed to whitewash it
24. Murderer: ___ Joe
25. Tom gave some to Peter, making him act crazy: ___ killer

Tom Sawyer Crossword 3

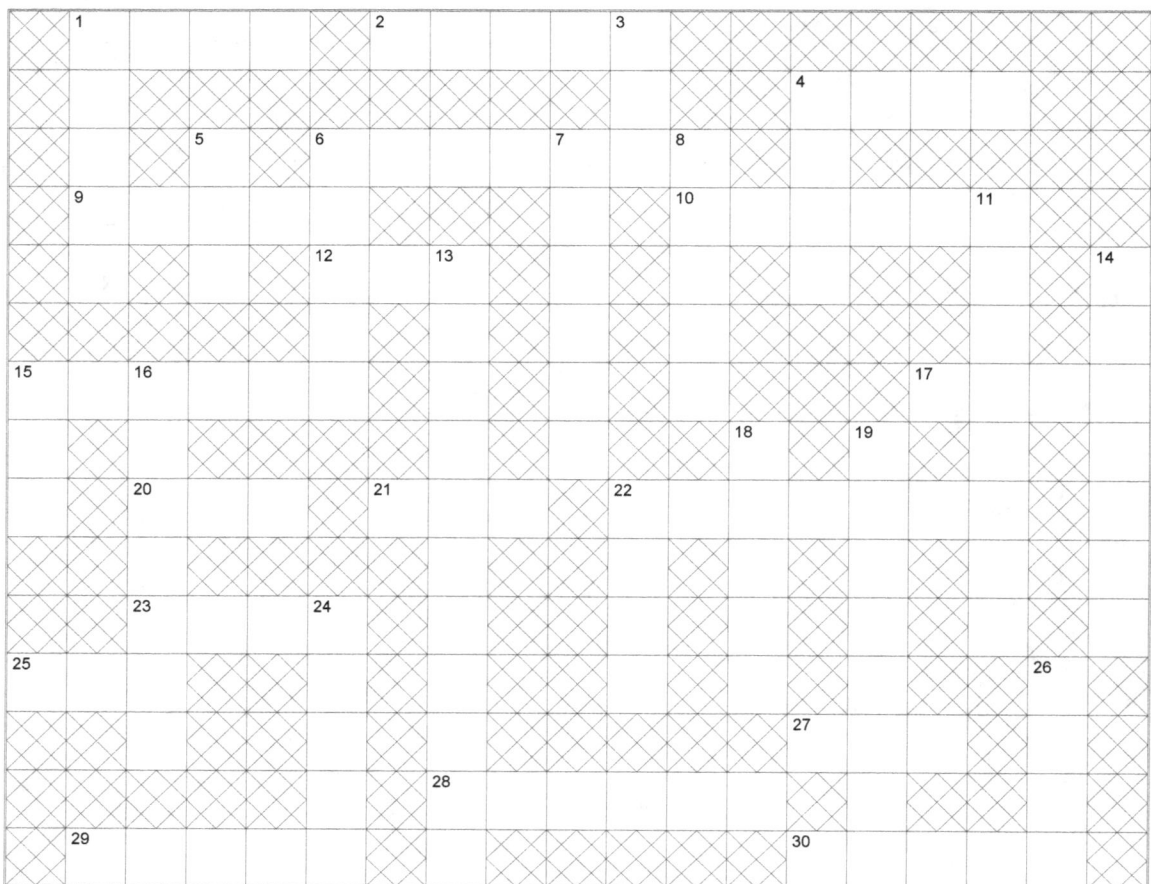

Across
1. Dead ones are good for curing warts.
2. Place where the trial is held
4. Becky tore the teacher's
6. They wore fancy clothes.
9. Tom was supposed to whitewash it
10. What Tom and Huck witnessed in the graveyard
12. He took the blame for tearing the teacher's book.
15. Tom's last name
17. Huck's last name
20. Number __
21. The boys stole Mr. Dobbins's
22. AKA Twain
23. Son of the town drunk
25. Went to island with Huck and Tom
27. Tom had been engaged to her before Becky.
28. Muff; drunk accused of murder
29. The boys left it and the pick downstairs.
30. Murderer: ___ Joe

Down
1. Tom got these and kisses from Aunt Polly upon his return.
3. Tom had a sore one.
4. Tom's notepaper
5. It spilled on Tom's spelling book.
6. The cat
7. How Tom got his tickets
8. Huck taught Tom & Joe how to do this bad habit.
11. Doctor Injun Joe killed
13. The river
14. The boys attended their own
15. Tom's half-brother
16. Tom blamed the unsuccessful marble spell on these.
18. She was engaged to Tom.
19. He saved Widow Douglas.
22. Place where Tom and Becky got lost
24. A gory one was found next to Dr. Robinson
26. Tom gave some to Peter, making him act crazy: ___ killer

Tom Sawyer Crossword 3 Answer Key

	1 C	A	T	S		2 C	O	U	R	3 T				
	U									O		4 B	O	O	K
	F	5 I		6 P	I	R	A	7 T	E	8 S		A		
	9 F	E	N	C	E			R		10 M	U	R	D	11 R	
		S	K	12 T	O	13 M	A			O		K		O	14 F
				E		I		D		K				B	U
15 S	A	16 W	Y	E	R		S	E		E			17 F	I	N	N
I		I				S		D			18 B		19 W	N		E
D		20 T	W	O		21 W	I	G		22 C	L	E	M	E	N	S	R
		C				S				A		C		L	O		A
		23 H	U	24 K		S				V		K		S	N		L
25 J	O	E		N		I				E		Y		H		26 P	
		S		I		P						27 A	M	Y		A	
				F		28 P	O	T	T	E	R		A			I	
		29 S	P	A	D	E						30 I	N	J	U	N	

Across
1. Dead ones are good for curing warts.
2. Place where the trial is held
4. Becky tore the teacher's
6. They wore fancy clothes.
9. Tom was supposed to whitewash it
10. What Tom and Huck witnessed in the graveyard
12. He took the blame for tearing the teacher's book.
15. Tom's last name
17. Huck's last name
20. Number __
21. The boys stole Mr. Dobbins's
22. AKA Twain
23. Son of the town drunk
25. Went to island with Huck and Tom
27. Tom had been engaged to her before Becky.
28. Muff; drunk accused of murder
29. The boys left it and the pick downstairs.
30. Murderer: ___ Joe

Down
1. Tom got these and kisses from Aunt Polly upon his return.
3. Tom had a sore one.
4. Tom's notepaper
5. It spilled on Tom's spelling book.
6. The cat
7. How Tom got his tickets
8. Huck taught Tom & Joe how to do this bad habit.
11. Doctor Injun Joe killed
13. The river
14. The boys attended their own
15. Tom's half-brother
16. Tom blamed the unsuccessful marble spell on these.
18. She was engaged to Tom.
19. He saved Widow Douglas.
22. Place where Tom and Becky got lost
24. A gory one was found next to Dr. Robinson
26. Tom gave some to Peter, making him act crazy: ___ killer

Tom Sawyer Crossword 4

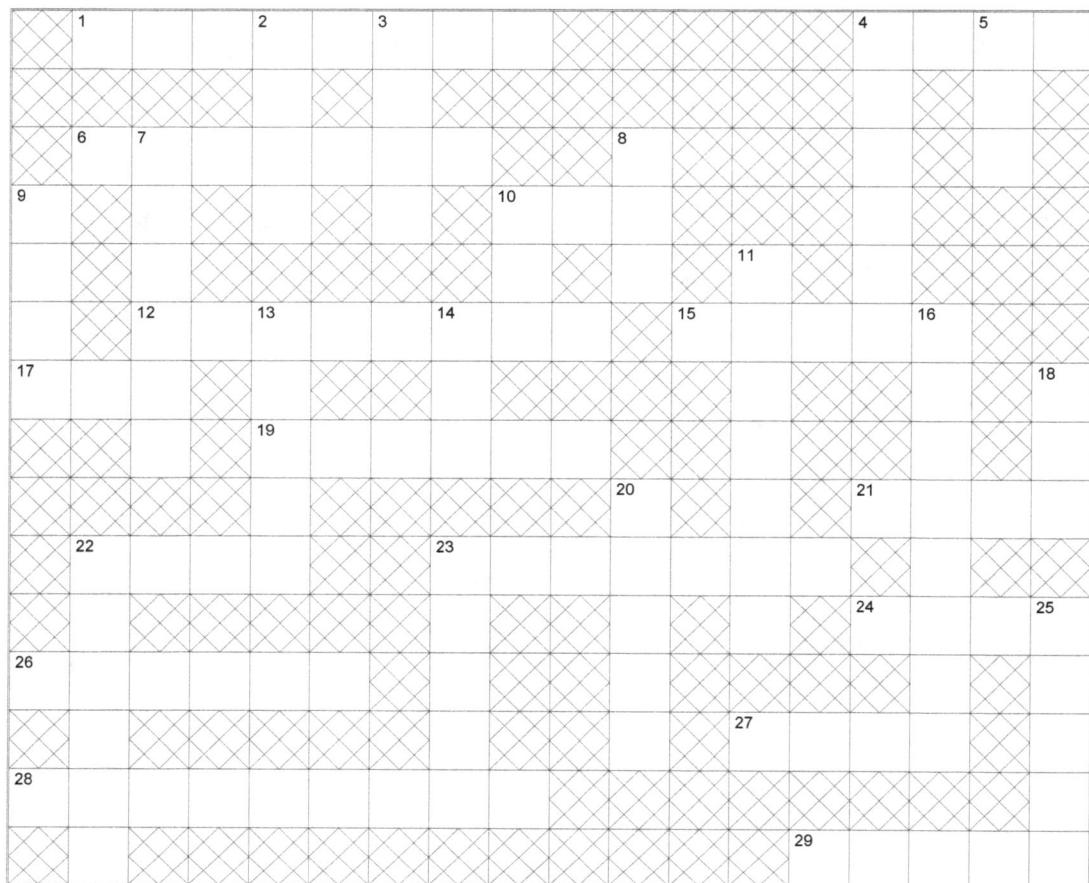

Across
1. Tom passed time in church by watching this.
4. Tom gave some to Peter, making him act crazy: ___ killer
6. Sunday school superintendent
10. He took the blame for tearing the teacher's book.
12. Doctor Injun Joe killed
15. Place where the trial is held
17. Tom had a sore one.
19. Tom blew out Becky's to conserve.
21. Group of boys; Tom Sawyer's ___
22. Tom's girl cousin
23. The boys attended their own
24. Son of the town drunk
26. How Tom got his tickets
27. Place where Tom and Becky got lost
28. Tom's name was printed in it for telling on Injun Joe
29. Huck taught Tom & Joe how to do this bad habit.

Down
2. Dead ones are good for curing warts.
3. Tom's notepaper
4. Muff; drunk accused of murder
5. It spilled on Tom's spelling book.
7. New boy; spilled ink on Tom's book
8. Tom had been engaged to her before Becky.
9. Tom could do this through the gap in his teeth.
10. Number __
11. The widow
13. She was engaged to Tom.
14. Tom's half-brother
16. You have to dig for it where the shadow of a dead tree limb falls at midnight.
18. The boys stole Mr. Dobbins's
20. The cat
22. What Tom and Huck witnessed in the graveyard
23. Tom was supposed to whitewash it
25. A gory one was found next to Dr. Robinson

Tom Sawyer Crossword 4 Answer Key

	1 P	I	N	2 C	H	3 B	U	G			4 P	A	5 N
				A		A					O		N
	6 W	7 A	L	T	E	R	S		8 A		T		K
9 S		L		S		K		10 T	O	M	T		
P		F				W		Y		11 D	E		
I		12 R	O	13 B	I	14 N	S	O	N	15 C	O	U	R	16 T
17 T	O	E		E		I				U			R		18 W
		D		19 C	A	N	D	L	E		G		E		I
				K					20 P		L	21 G	A	N	G
	22 M	A	R	Y		23 F	U	N	E	R	A	L	S		
	U					E			T			24 H	U	C	25 K
26 T	R	A	D	E	D		N		E			R		N
	D					C			R		27 C	A	V	E	I
28 N	E	W	S	P	A	P	E	R					F
	R									29 S	M	O	K	E

Across
1. Tom passed time in church by watching this.
4. Tom gave some to Peter, making him act crazy: ___ killer
6. Sunday school superintendent
10. He took the blame for tearing the teacher's book.
12. Doctor Injun Joe killed
15. Place where the trial is held
17. Tom had a sore one.
19. Tom blew out Becky's to conserve.
21. Group of boys; Tom Sawyer's ___
22. Tom's girl cousin
23. The boys attended their own
24. Son of the town drunk
26. How Tom got his tickets
27. Place where Tom and Becky got lost
28. Tom's name was printed in it for telling on Injun Joe
29. Huck taught Tom & Joe how to do this bad habit.

Down
2. Dead ones are good for curing warts.
3. Tom's notepaper
4. Muff; drunk accused of murder
5. It spilled on Tom's spelling book.
7. New boy; spilled ink on Tom's book
8. Tom had been engaged to her before Becky.
9. Tom could do this through the gap in his teeth.
10. Number ___
11. The widow
13. She was engaged to Tom.
14. Tom's half-brother
16. You have to dig for it where the shadow of a dead tree limb falls at midnight.
18. The boys stole Mr. Dobbins's
20. The cat
22. What Tom and Huck witnessed in the graveyard
23. Tom was supposed to whitewash it
25. A gory one was found next to Dr. Robinson

Tom Sawyer

COURT	PAIN	CONSCIENCE	FENCE	PETER
ALFRED	TICKETS	MARY	KNIFE	PINCHBUG
TOM	CATS	FREE SPACE	SID	FUNERAL
MURDER	POLLY	PETERSBURG	AMY	BARK
CAVE	TWAIN	GANG	WITNESS	HOUSE

Tom Sawyer

TREASURE	JOE	NEWSPAPER	SAWYER	INJUN
WALTERS	DOBBINS	INK	FISH	FINN
SPADE	MISSISSIPPI	FREE SPACE	BOOK	CANDLE
DOUGLAS	ROBINSON	TRADED	SMOKE	WITCHES
PIRATES	JACKSON	BECKY	TOE	TWO

Tom Sawyer

INK	PETERSBURG	MARY	TICKETS	TRADED
BARK	JACKSON	WELSHMAN	SPIT	DOUGLAS
WIG	ALFRED	FREE SPACE	BECKY	GANG
BOOK	SKIFF	SPADE	ROBINSON	SAWYER
FINN	CANDLE	NEWSPAPER	CONSCIENCE	CAVE

Tom Sawyer

POLLY	FUNERAL	FENCE	SID	HUCK
COURT	DOBBINS	PIRATES	FISH	CLEMENS
TOE	MURDER	FREE SPACE	WITNESS	CATS
TWO	TOM	POTTER	TREASURE	WITCHES
CUFFS	TRAPPED	THATCHER	INJUN	PINCHBUG

Tom Sawyer

SKIFF	PAIN	FINN	HOUSE	TWAIN
AMY	BOOK	TRADED	WITCHES	CAVE
ALFRED	TOM	FREE SPACE	JOE	CATS
THATCHER	NEWSPAPER	ROBINSON	MARY	TICKETS
TOE	FISH	FUNERAL	TRAPPED	WIG

Tom Sawyer

CUFFS	POTTER	COURT	FENCE	BECKY
PINCHBUG	WITNESS	WALTERS	PETERSBURG	SPADE
POLLY	SID	FREE SPACE	INJUN	SMOKE
MURDER	WELSHMAN	DOUGLAS	TREASURE	JACKSON
MISSISSIPPI	CLEMENS	CANDLE	KNIFE	DOBBINS

Tom Sawyer

TWAIN	COURT	TICKETS	MURDER	MISSISSIPPI
THATCHER	WELSHMAN	FISH	CANDLE	WITCHES
JOE	TRAPPED	FREE SPACE	TWO	PETERSBURG
FINN	WALTERS	POTTER	DOBBINS	INK
MARY	JACKSON	HOUSE	SID	TOE

Tom Sawyer

FUNERAL	PETER	CONSCIENCE	NEWSPAPER	SPADE
INJUN	ROBINSON	SKIFF	BARK	PIRATES
FENCE	WITNESS	FREE SPACE	DOUGLAS	CUFFS
CATS	CAVE	GANG	AMY	BECKY
SMOKE	TOM	BOOK	CLEMENS	SPIT

Tom Sawyer

BECKY	CONSCIENCE	WITCHES	PETERSBURG	MURDER
TICKETS	WITNESS	SKIFF	CAVE	SAWYER
TOM	BOOK	FREE SPACE	CANDLE	CATS
BARK	PAIN	SPADE	THATCHER	HUCK
TREASURE	HOUSE	GANG	WALTERS	FINN

Tom Sawyer

TWAIN	DOBBINS	PIRATES	JACKSON	SID
INK	TRADED	TOE	MISSISSIPPI	FENCE
FUNERAL	WELSHMAN	FREE SPACE	SMOKE	POTTER
FISH	CUFFS	JOE	INJUN	AMY
NEWSPAPER	KNIFE	DOUGLAS	CLEMENS	ALFRED

Tom Sawyer

BOOK	WIG	GANG	FINN	KNIFE
PAIN	CONSCIENCE	MISSISSIPPI	HUCK	TOE
TOM	PINCHBUG	FREE SPACE	FISH	FENCE
CAVE	WITNESS	DOBBINS	SAWYER	SPADE
JACKSON	INK	SMOKE	MARY	TICKETS

Tom Sawyer

BECKY	COURT	AMY	PETERSBURG	SKIFF
BARK	TWO	TWAIN	POTTER	MURDER
PIRATES	WELSHMAN	FREE SPACE	JOE	WALTERS
DOUGLAS	TRAPPED	PETER	HOUSE	ROBINSON
CUFFS	FUNERAL	ALFRED	THATCHER	POLLY

Tom Sawyer

CONSCIENCE	PIRATES	FENCE	TRADED	COURT
CAVE	ALFRED	NEWSPAPER	SMOKE	PETER
HUCK	WITNESS	FREE SPACE	SID	INJUN
FISH	DOBBINS	WELSHMAN	TWAIN	JOE
CATS	TICKETS	MURDER	MISSISSIPPI	BOOK

Tom Sawyer

PINCHBUG	TOE	SPIT	POLLY	CLEMENS
THATCHER	SKIFF	FINN	WALTERS	SPADE
ROBINSON	WIG	FREE SPACE	INK	AMY
FUNERAL	TOM	SAWYER	CANDLE	BARK
JACKSON	PAIN	DOUGLAS	POTTER	BECKY

Tom Sawyer

PIRATES	TRADED	NEWSPAPER	TWAIN	TREASURE
BARK	PAIN	MARY	WELSHMAN	INJUN
WITNESS	COURT	FREE SPACE	KNIFE	JACKSON
FENCE	TOE	BECKY	GANG	SAWYER
FINN	HUCK	CATS	SID	CUFFS

Tom Sawyer

POLLY	AMY	SPADE	SKIFF	SPIT
CANDLE	TRAPPED	PINCHBUG	HOUSE	DOBBINS
TOM	DOUGLAS	FREE SPACE	WALTERS	POTTER
INK	ALFRED	PETERSBURG	CONSCIENCE	WITCHES
TICKETS	WIG	FUNERAL	ROBINSON	CLEMENS

Tom Sawyer

WELSHMAN	CATS	COURT	DOUGLAS	POLLY
HOUSE	TOM	SMOKE	MISSISSIPPI	TOE
PIRATES	WALTERS	FREE SPACE	NEWSPAPER	SAWYER
INJUN	SPADE	TICKETS	SPIT	JACKSON
INK	FUNERAL	JOE	FISH	WITCHES

Tom Sawyer

WIG	HUCK	TRAPPED	THATCHER	CANDLE
AMY	TWAIN	PINCHBUG	MARY	BARK
ALFRED	SKIFF	FREE SPACE	BECKY	BOOK
CAVE	POTTER	TWO	WITNESS	FINN
PETER	FENCE	DOBBINS	KNIFE	TREASURE

Tom Sawyer

COURT	HUCK	WIG	FINN	TICKETS
BOOK	CAVE	WALTERS	MISSISSIPPI	INJUN
CATS	FISH	FREE SPACE	SKIFF	TOM
POTTER	SPADE	PETER	DOBBINS	PAIN
WITNESS	MURDER	TWAIN	BECKY	TRADED

Tom Sawyer

SAWYER	TWO	CANDLE	POLLY	CUFFS
JACKSON	WELSHMAN	KNIFE	PINCHBUG	GANG
DOUGLAS	INK	FREE SPACE	AMY	CLEMENS
ROBINSON	CONSCIENCE	JOE	SID	FUNERAL
TRAPPED	SPIT	PETERSBURG	SMOKE	WITCHES

Tom Sawyer

SPIT	WALTERS	ALFRED	JACKSON	HOUSE
POLLY	AMY	THATCHER	FENCE	SMOKE
PETERSBURG	CUFFS	FREE SPACE	CATS	CAVE
TWO	TWAIN	WITCHES	GANG	CONSCIENCE
TRAPPED	INK	NEWSPAPER	INJUN	COURT

Tom Sawyer

TRADED	POTTER	PAIN	FINN	TOE
SID	WITNESS	MARY	CLEMENS	TREASURE
ROBINSON	SAWYER	FREE SPACE	JOE	DOUGLAS
HUCK	FISH	BOOK	DOBBINS	SPADE
MURDER	BARK	PETER	PINCHBUG	SKIFF

Tom Sawyer

TWAIN	WITNESS	SMOKE	DOBBINS	BOOK
COURT	PIRATES	WELSHMAN	NEWSPAPER	TOE
POLLY	SKIFF	FREE SPACE	TREASURE	WALTERS
FUNERAL	FINN	FISH	CANDLE	INK
KNIFE	MURDER	JACKSON	BECKY	WIG

Tom Sawyer

TRADED	WITCHES	JOE	POTTER	PETERSBURG
TOM	FENCE	BARK	GANG	THATCHER
INJUN	PETER	FREE SPACE	ROBINSON	HOUSE
CLEMENS	TICKETS	MISSISSIPPI	CAVE	MARY
SPADE	SAWYER	TWO	DOUGLAS	PAIN

Tom Sawyer

PIRATES	JOE	SKIFF	AMY	PETER
BARK	CONSCIENCE	MISSISSIPPI	CATS	HOUSE
PETERSBURG	INK	FREE SPACE	TRAPPED	TREASURE
MARY	TOM	BECKY	SID	SAWYER
POLLY	THATCHER	CANDLE	CAVE	TRADED

Tom Sawyer

CLEMENS	ALFRED	COURT	TICKETS	MURDER
POTTER	FUNERAL	FENCE	TOE	INJUN
PAIN	FISH	FREE SPACE	WIG	TWO
WITNESS	CUFFS	FINN	SPADE	WITCHES
PINCHBUG	SPIT	WELSHMAN	NEWSPAPER	HUCK

Tom Sawyer

SPIT	CAVE	DOBBINS	BECKY	TOE
TICKETS	PAIN	MARY	BARK	CANDLE
BOOK	KNIFE	FREE SPACE	HOUSE	WIG
NEWSPAPER	WITNESS	DOUGLAS	JACKSON	CONSCIENCE
TWAIN	TREASURE	FUNERAL	COURT	CUFFS

Tom Sawyer

JOE	INK	PETER	WITCHES	WALTERS
SAWYER	CATS	POLLY	FENCE	TOM
MURDER	SKIFF	FREE SPACE	POTTER	SPADE
PIRATES	TWO	SMOKE	FINN	FISH
ALFRED	SID	WELSHMAN	INJUN	PETERSBURG

Tom Sawyer

WALTERS	TOM	HUCK	POLLY	BOOK
FISH	DOUGLAS	FINN	CLEMENS	WITNESS
INK	WITCHES	FREE SPACE	TRADED	NEWSPAPER
WIG	PINCHBUG	MISSISSIPPI	ROBINSON	JACKSON
CATS	KNIFE	HOUSE	SKIFF	BARK

Tom Sawyer

CAVE	PIRATES	WELSHMAN	GANG	MARY
THATCHER	TOE	MURDER	SPADE	PAIN
TRAPPED	TICKETS	FREE SPACE	TWO	PETER
ALFRED	CONSCIENCE	POTTER	DOBBINS	SID
SPIT	COURT	FENCE	CANDLE	SAWYER

Tom Sawyer

CUFFS	SAWYER	TWAIN	SPIT	SKIFF
CLEMENS	PIRATES	WITCHES	FUNERAL	CANDLE
FISH	ROBINSON	FREE SPACE	BOOK	SID
WIG	WITNESS	SPADE	MURDER	POTTER
PINCHBUG	SMOKE	ALFRED	FINN	GANG

Tom Sawyer

PETER	TRADED	WALTERS	CAVE	FENCE
TICKETS	AMY	POLLY	BARK	PAIN
INJUN	JACKSON	FREE SPACE	THATCHER	TOE
TRAPPED	PETERSBURG	HUCK	JOE	MARY
TWO	NEWSPAPER	COURT	WELSHMAN	MISSISSIPPI

Tom Sawyer Vocabulary Word List

No.	Word	Clue/Definition
1.	ABASHED	Ashamed; uneasy; disconcerted
2.	ABSTAIN	Stop doing something by one's own choice
3.	ALACRITY	Eagerness
4.	APPEASED	Calmed; satisfied; pacified
5.	APPREHENSIVELY	Anxiously; with reservation
6.	ASSENT	Agreement
7.	ATTRITION	A gradual rubbing away or wearing down
8.	AVERTED	Turned away
9.	AWED	Amazed with mixed emotions of reverence, respect, and dread
10.	BLISS	Extreme happiness
11.	CARICATURE	Drawing in which the subjects distinctive traits are exaggerated
12.	CEASED	Stopped
13.	CHAOS	Disorder; confusion
14.	COGITATING	Thinking
15.	CONDESCEND	Lower one's self to the position of inferiors
16.	CONSENT	Agree to do something
17.	CONTRIVED	Schemed
18.	COUNTENANCE	Face
19.	COVET	Want
20.	DAUNTLESS	Fearless
21.	DERISION	Ridicule
22.	DISDAIN	Contempt
23.	ELOQUENT	Characterized by persuasive, powerful, or moving words
24.	FRESCOED	Painted
25.	IMPAIRED	Damaged; diminished in strength
26.	IMPERISHABLE	Indestructible
27.	IMPLORE	Beg
28.	INGENIOUS	Clever; inventive
29.	INQUEST	Judicial inquiry into the cause of a death
30.	INVARIABLY	Without change
31.	MAGNANIMOUS	Courageously noble
32.	MELANCHOLY	Depressed; sad; gloomy
33.	MUTUAL	Possessed in common
34.	ODIOUS	Arousing a strong dislike or displeasure
35.	OPPRESSIVE	Difficult to bear
36.	PALLID	Pale; dull; lifeless
37.	PERPLEXED	Puzzled; uncertain
38.	PERVADING	Present throughout
39.	PLAUSIBLE	Believable
40.	PRECARIOUS	Dangerously lacking in security or stability
41.	PRECIPICE	Overhanging rock; cliff
42.	PRODIGIOUS	Impressively great
43.	RESOLUTION	Determination
44.	SEAR	Burn; scorch
45.	SMOTE	Inflicted a heavy blow upon
46.	SUBDUED	Conquered and brought under control
47.	SUPPLICATION	A plea
48.	TEDIOUS	Tiresome by reason of extreme length or slowness
49.	TYRANNY	A ruler's unjust use of power
50.	UNPALATABLE	Unacceptable to the mind or senses
51.	UPBRAID	Reprimand

Tom Sawyer Vocabulary Word List Continued

No.	Word	Clue/Definition
52.	VAIN	Excessively proud
53.	VICE	Bad habit
54.	WARY	Cautious

Tom Sawyer Vocabulary Fill In The Blanks 1

_____ 1. Determination

_____ 2. Agreement

_____ 3. Disorder; confusion

_____ 4. Thinking

_____ 5. Present throughout

_____ 6. A gradual rubbing away or wearing down

_____ 7. Painted

_____ 8. Stopped

_____ 9. Calmed; satisfied; pacified

_____ 10. A plea

_____ 11. Puzzled; uncertain

_____ 12. Damaged; diminished in strength

_____ 13. Depressed; sad; gloomy

_____ 14. Dangerously lacking in security or stability

_____ 15. Ashamed; uneasy; disconcerted

_____ 16. Unacceptable to the mind or senses

_____ 17. Impressively great

_____ 18. Tiresome by reason of extreme length or slowness

_____ 19. Overhanging rock; cliff

_____ 20. Pale; dull; lifeless

Tom Sawyer Vocabulary Fill In The Blanks 1 Answer Key

RESOLUTION	1. Determination
ASSENT	2. Agreement
CHAOS	3. Disorder; confusion
COGITATING	4. Thinking
PERVADING	5. Present throughout
ATTRITION	6. A gradual rubbing away or wearing down
FRESCOED	7. Painted
CEASED	8. Stopped
APPEASED	9. Calmed; satisfied; pacified
SUPPLICATION	10. A plea
PERPLEXED	11. Puzzled; uncertain
IMPAIRED	12. Damaged; diminished in strength
MELANCHOLY	13. Depressed; sad; gloomy
PRECARIOUS	14. Dangerously lacking in security or stability
ABASHED	15. Ashamed; uneasy; disconcerted
UNPALATABLE	16. Unacceptable to the mind or senses
PRODIGIOUS	17. Impressively great
TEDIOUS	18. Tiresome by reason of extreme length or slowness
PRECIPICE	19. Overhanging rock; cliff
PALLID	20. Pale; dull; lifeless

Tom Sawyer Vocabulary Fill In The Blanks 2

_____ 1. Indestructible

_____ 2. Burn; scorch

_____ 3. Courageously noble

_____ 4. Inflicted a heavy blow upon

_____ 5. Turned away

_____ 6. Impressively great

_____ 7. Excessively proud

_____ 8. Conquered and brought under control

_____ 9. Want

_____ 10. Ashamed; uneasy; disconcerted

_____ 11. Stop doing something by one's own choice

_____ 12. Reprimand

_____ 13. Tiresome by reason of extreme length or slowness

_____ 14. Agree to do something

_____ 15. Difficult to bear

_____ 16. Schemed

_____ 17. Puzzled; uncertain

_____ 18. Agreement

_____ 19. Extreme happiness

_____ 20. Drawing in which the subjects distinctive traits are exaggerated

Tom Sawyer Vocabulary Fill In The Blanks 2 Answer Key

IMPERISHABLE	1. Indestructible
SEAR	2. Burn; scorch
MAGNANIMOUS	3. Courageously noble
SMOTE	4. Inflicted a heavy blow upon
AVERTED	5. Turned away
PRODIGIOUS	6. Impressively great
VAIN	7. Excessively proud
SUBDUED	8. Conquered and brought under control
COVET	9. Want
ABASHED	10. Ashamed; uneasy; disconcerted
ABSTAIN	11. Stop doing something by one's own choice
UPBRAID	12. Reprimand
TEDIOUS	13. Tiresome by reason of extreme length or slowness
CONSENT	14. Agree to do something
OPPRESSIVE	15. Difficult to bear
CONTRIVED	16. Schemed
PERPLEXED	17. Puzzled; uncertain
ASSENT	18. Agreement
BLISS	19. Extreme happiness
CARICATURE	20. Drawing in which the subjects distinctive traits are exaggerated

Tom Sawyer Vocabulary Fill In The Blanks 3

_____ 1. Present throughout

_____ 2. Characterized by persuasive, powerful, or moving words

_____ 3. Anxiously; with reservation

_____ 4. Beg

_____ 5. Drawing in which the subjects distinctive traits are exaggerated

_____ 6. Impressively great

_____ 7. Face

_____ 8. Calmed; satisfied; pacified

_____ 9. Damaged; diminished in strength

_____ 10. Puzzled; uncertain

_____ 11. Pale; dull; lifeless

_____ 12. Fearless

_____ 13. Cautious

_____ 14. Overhanging rock; cliff

_____ 15. Turned away

_____ 16. Without change

_____ 17. Bad habit

_____ 18. Eagerness

_____ 19. Ashamed; uneasy; disconcerted

_____ 20. Stopped

Tom Sawyer Vocabulary Fill In The Blanks 3 Answer Key

PERVADING	1.	Present throughout
ELOQUENT	2.	Characterized by persuasive, powerful, or moving words
APPREHENSIVELY	3.	Anxiously; with reservation
IMPLORE	4.	Beg
CARICATURE	5.	Drawing in which the subjects distinctive traits are exaggerated
PRODIGIOUS	6.	Impressively great
COUNTENANCE	7.	Face
APPEASED	8.	Calmed; satisfied; pacified
IMPAIRED	9.	Damaged; diminished in strength
PERPLEXED	10.	Puzzled; uncertain
PALLID	11.	Pale; dull; lifeless
DAUNTLESS	12.	Fearless
WARY	13.	Cautious
PRECIPICE	14.	Overhanging rock; cliff
AVERTED	15.	Turned away
INVARIABLY	16.	Without change
VICE	17.	Bad habit
ALACRITY	18.	Eagerness
ABASHED	19.	Ashamed; uneasy; disconcerted
CEASED	20.	Stopped

Tom Sawyer Vocabulary Fill In The Blanks 4

1. Fearless
2. Eagerness
3. Arousing a strong dislike or displeasure
4. Thinking
5. Puzzled; uncertain
6. A gradual rubbing away or wearing down
7. Indestructible
8. Burn; scorch
9. Lower one's self to the position of inferiors
10. Calmed; satisfied; pacified
11. Unacceptable to the mind or senses
12. Impressively great
13. Present throughout
14. Determination
15. Disorder; confusion
16. A plea
17. Pale; dull; lifeless
18. Face
19. Ashamed; uneasy; disconcerted
20. Inflicted a heavy blow upon

Tom Sawyer Vocabulary Fill In The Blanks 4 Answer Key

DAUNTLESS	1. Fearless
ALACRITY	2. Eagerness
ODIOUS	3. Arousing a strong dislike or displeasure
COGITATING	4. Thinking
PERPLEXED	5. Puzzled; uncertain
ATTRITION	6. A gradual rubbing away or wearing down
IMPERISHABLE	7. Indestructible
SEAR	8. Burn; scorch
CONDESCEND	9. Lower one's self to the position of inferiors
APPEASED	10. Calmed; satisfied; pacified
UNPALATABLE	11. Unacceptable to the mind or senses
PRODIGIOUS	12. Impressively great
PERVADING	13. Present throughout
RESOLUTION	14. Determination
CHAOS	15. Disorder; confusion
SUPPLICATION	16. A plea
PALLID	17. Pale; dull; lifeless
COUNTENANCE	18. Face
ABASHED	19. Ashamed; uneasy; disconcerted
SMOTE	20. Inflicted a heavy blow upon

Tom Sawyer Vocabulary Matching 1

___ 1. CONSENT
___ 2. IMPAIRED
___ 3. PERVADING
___ 4. PRODIGIOUS
___ 5. AWED
___ 6. MAGNANIMOUS
___ 7. COUNTENANCE
___ 8. BLISS
___ 9. UNPALATABLE
___ 10. APPEASED
___ 11. SUBDUED
___ 12. ABASHED
___ 13. CONTRIVED
___ 14. SMOTE
___ 15. INVARIABLY
___ 16. ABSTAIN
___ 17. INQUEST
___ 18. TEDIOUS
___ 19. DAUNTLESS
___ 20. CEASED
___ 21. MUTUAL
___ 22. CONDESCEND
___ 23. IMPERISHABLE
___ 24. PALLID
___ 25. PLAUSIBLE

A. Inflicted a heavy blow upon
B. Pale; dull; lifeless
C. Unacceptable to the mind or senses
D. Impressively great
E. Agree to do something
F. Amazed with mixed emotions of reverence, respect, and dread
G. Stop doing something by one's own choice
H. Schemed
I. Face
J. Tiresome by reason of extreme length or slowness
K. Judicial inquiry into the cause of a death
L. Believable
M. Stopped
N. Without change
O. Possessed in common
P. Ashamed; uneasy; disconcerted
Q. Damaged; diminished in strength
R. Lower one's self to the position of inferiors
S. Courageously noble
T. Indestructible
U. Fearless
V. Calmed; satisfied; pacified
W. Conquered and brought under control
X. Extreme happiness
Y. Present throughout

Tom Sawyer Vocabulary Matching 1 Answer Key

E - 1. CONSENT A. Inflicted a heavy blow upon
Q - 2. IMPAIRED B. Pale; dull; lifeless
Y - 3. PERVADING C. Unacceptable to the mind or senses
D - 4. PRODIGIOUS D. Impressively great
F - 5. AWED E. Agree to do something
S - 6. MAGNANIMOUS F. Amazed with mixed emotions of reverence, respect, and dread
I - 7. COUNTENANCE G. Stop doing something by one's own choice
X - 8. BLISS H. Schemed
C - 9. UNPALATABLE I. Face
V - 10. APPEASED J. Tiresome by reason of extreme length or slowness
W - 11. SUBDUED K. Judicial inquiry into the cause of a death
P - 12. ABASHED L. Believable
H - 13. CONTRIVED M. Stopped
A - 14. SMOTE N. Without change
N - 15. INVARIABLY O. Possessed in common
G - 16. ABSTAIN P. Ashamed; uneasy; disconcerted
K - 17. INQUEST Q. Damaged; diminished in strength
J - 18. TEDIOUS R. Lower one's self to the position of inferiors
U - 19. DAUNTLESS S. Courageously noble
M - 20. CEASED T. Indestructible
O - 21. MUTUAL U. Fearless
R - 22. CONDESCEND V. Calmed; satisfied; pacified
T - 23. IMPERISHABLE W. Conquered and brought under control
B - 24. PALLID X. Extreme happiness
L - 25. PLAUSIBLE Y. Present throughout

Tom Sawyer Vocabulary Matching 2

___ 1. ATTRITION
___ 2. CHAOS
___ 3. CONDESCEND
___ 4. CARICATURE
___ 5. DERISION
___ 6. TEDIOUS
___ 7. ABASHED
___ 8. CEASED
___ 9. AWED
___10. VICE
___11. MAGNANIMOUS
___12. TYRANNY
___13. PALLID
___14. PRODIGIOUS
___15. COVET
___16. DISDAIN
___17. WARY
___18. INVARIABLY
___19. ABSTAIN
___20. COUNTENANCE
___21. ODIOUS
___22. SMOTE
___23. CONTRIVED
___24. PERVADING
___25. IMPERISHABLE

A. Impressively great
B. Drawing in which the subjects distinctive traits are exaggerated
C. Bad habit
D. Stop doing something by one's own choice
E. Inflicted a heavy blow upon
F. Ashamed; uneasy; disconcerted
G. Face
H. Present throughout
I. Schemed
J. Indestructible
K. Contempt
L. Courageously noble
M. Without change
N. Ridicule
O. Cautious
P. Lower one's self to the position of inferiors
Q. Amazed with mixed emotions of reverence, respect, and dread
R. Stopped
S. Arousing a strong dislike or displeasure
T. Tiresome by reason of extreme length or slowness
U. Want
V. A ruler's unjust use of power
W. Pale; dull; lifeless
X. Disorder; confusion
Y. A gradual rubbing away or wearing down

Tom Sawyer Vocabulary Matching 2 Answer Key

Y - 1. ATTRITION		A. Impressively great
X - 2. CHAOS		B. Drawing in which the subjects distinctive traits are exaggerated
P - 3. CONDESCEND		C. Bad habit
B - 4. CARICATURE		D. Stop doing something by one's own choice
N - 5. DERISION		E. Inflicted a heavy blow upon
T - 6. TEDIOUS		F. Ashamed; uneasy; disconcerted
F - 7. ABASHED		G. Face
R - 8. CEASED		H. Present throughout
Q - 9. AWED		I. Schemed
C - 10. VICE		J. Indestructible
L - 11. MAGNANIMOUS		K. Contempt
V - 12. TYRANNY		L. Courageously noble
W - 13. PALLID		M. Without change
A - 14. PRODIGIOUS		N. Ridicule
U - 15. COVET		O. Cautious
K - 16. DISDAIN		P. Lower one's self to the position of inferiors
O - 17. WARY		Q. Amazed with mixed emotions of reverence, respect, and dread
M - 18. INVARIABLY		R. Stopped
D - 19. ABSTAIN		S. Arousing a strong dislike or displeasure
G - 20. COUNTENANCE		T. Tiresome by reason of extreme length or slowness
S - 21. ODIOUS		U. Want
E - 22. SMOTE		V. A ruler's unjust use of power
I - 23. CONTRIVED		W. Pale; dull; lifeless
H - 24. PERVADING		X. Disorder; confusion
J - 25. IMPERISHABLE		Y. A gradual rubbing away or wearing down

Tom Sawyer Vocabulary Matching 3

___ 1. MELANCHOLY   A. Unacceptable to the mind or senses
___ 2. DERISION   B. Turned away
___ 3. INVARIABLY   C. Painted
___ 4. UPBRAID   D. Anxiously; with reservation
___ 5. APPREHENSIVELY   E. Present throughout
___ 6. VICE   F. Inflicted a heavy blow upon
___ 7. ALACRITY   G. Stop doing something by one's own choice
___ 8. CONTRIVED   H. Disorder; confusion
___ 9. FRESCOED   I. Without change
___ 10. WARY   J. A ruler's unjust use of power
___ 11. AVERTED   K. Eagerness
___ 12. TYRANNY   L. Depressed; sad; gloomy
___ 13. ABSTAIN   M. Contempt
___ 14. IMPAIRED   N. Ridicule
___ 15. PERVADING   O. Extreme happiness
___ 16. CEASED   P. Possessed in common
___ 17. ASSENT   Q. Reprimand
___ 18. UNPALATABLE   R. Schemed
___ 19. PERPLEXED   S. Cautious
___ 20. DISDAIN   T. Damaged; diminished in strength
___ 21. BLISS   U. Agreement
___ 22. CHAOS   V. Bad habit
___ 23. PRECIPICE   W. Puzzled; uncertain
___ 24. MUTUAL   X. Overhanging rock; cliff
___ 25. SMOTE   Y. Stopped

Tom Sawyer Vocabulary Matching 3 Answer Key

L - 1.	MELANCHOLY	A. Unacceptable to the mind or senses
N - 2.	DERISION	B. Turned away
I - 3.	INVARIABLY	C. Painted
Q - 4.	UPBRAID	D. Anxiously; with reservation
D - 5.	APPREHENSIVELY	E. Present throughout
V - 6.	VICE	F. Inflicted a heavy blow upon
K - 7.	ALACRITY	G. Stop doing something by one's own choice
R - 8.	CONTRIVED	H. Disorder; confusion
C - 9.	FRESCOED	I. Without change
S - 10.	WARY	J. A ruler's unjust use of power
B - 11.	AVERTED	K. Eagerness
J - 12.	TYRANNY	L. Depressed; sad; gloomy
G - 13.	ABSTAIN	M. Contempt
T - 14.	IMPAIRED	N. Ridicule
E - 15.	PERVADING	O. Extreme happiness
Y - 16.	CEASED	P. Possessed in common
U - 17.	ASSENT	Q. Reprimand
A - 18.	UNPALATABLE	R. Schemed
W - 19.	PERPLEXED	S. Cautious
M - 20.	DISDAIN	T. Damaged; diminished in strength
O - 21.	BLISS	U. Agreement
H - 22.	CHAOS	V. Bad habit
X - 23.	PRECIPICE	W. Puzzled; uncertain
P - 24.	MUTUAL	X. Overhanging rock; cliff
F - 25.	SMOTE	Y. Stopped

Tom Sawyer Vocabulary Matching 4

___ 1. CEASED   A. Depressed; sad; gloomy
___ 2. COGITATING   B. Stopped
___ 3. APPEASED   C. Calmed; satisfied; pacified
___ 4. INQUEST   D. Want
___ 5. CONTRIVED   E. Agreement
___ 6. SUPPLICATION   F. Judicial inquiry into the cause of a death
___ 7. BLISS   G. Ridicule
___ 8. DERISION   H. Dangerously lacking in security or stability
___ 9. PLAUSIBLE   I. Tiresome by reason of extreme length or slowness
___10. APPREHENSIVELY J. Believable
___11. CHAOS   K. A plea
___12. SUBDUED   L. Thinking
___13. PRECARIOUS   M. Excessively proud
___14. OPPRESSIVE   N. Puzzled; uncertain
___15. PERPLEXED   O. Difficult to bear
___16. VAIN   P. Face
___17. COUNTENANCE   Q. Anxiously; with reservation
___18. MELANCHOLY   R. Conquered and brought under control
___19. ASSENT   S. Impressively great
___20. SEAR   T. Extreme happiness
___21. ODIOUS   U. Burn; scorch
___22. IMPAIRED   V. Schemed
___23. TEDIOUS   W. Damaged; diminished in strength
___24. COVET   X. Disorder; confusion
___25. PRODIGIOUS   Y. Arousing a strong dislike or displeasure

Tom Sawyer Vocabulary Matching 4 Answer Key

B - 1.	CEASED	A.	Depressed; sad; gloomy
L - 2.	COGITATING	B.	Stopped
C - 3.	APPEASED	C.	Calmed; satisfied; pacified
F - 4.	INQUEST	D.	Want
V - 5.	CONTRIVED	E.	Agreement
K - 6.	SUPPLICATION	F.	Judicial inquiry into the cause of a death
T - 7.	BLISS	G.	Ridicule
G - 8.	DERISION	H.	Dangerously lacking in security or stability
J - 9.	PLAUSIBLE	I.	Tiresome by reason of extreme length or slowness
Q - 10.	APPREHENSIVELY	J.	Believable
X - 11.	CHAOS	K.	A plea
R - 12.	SUBDUED	L.	Thinking
H - 13.	PRECARIOUS	M.	Excessively proud
O - 14.	OPPRESSIVE	N.	Puzzled; uncertain
N - 15.	PERPLEXED	O.	Difficult to bear
M - 16.	VAIN	P.	Face
P - 17.	COUNTENANCE	Q.	Anxiously; with reservation
A - 18.	MELANCHOLY	R.	Conquered and brought under control
E - 19.	ASSENT	S.	Impressively great
U - 20.	SEAR	T.	Extreme happiness
Y - 21.	ODIOUS	U.	Burn; scorch
W - 22.	IMPAIRED	V.	Schemed
I - 23.	TEDIOUS	W.	Damaged; diminished in strength
D - 24.	COVET	X.	Disorder; confusion
S - 25.	PRODIGIOUS	Y.	Arousing a strong dislike or displeasure

Tom Sawyer Vocabulary Magic Squares 1

Match the definition with the vocabulary word. Put your answers in the magic squares below. When your answers are correct, all columns and rows will add to the same number.

A. DAUNTLESS
B. INGENIOUS
C. CONDESCEND
D. WARY
E. ABASHED
F. FRESCOED
G. PALLID
H. ATTRITION
I. COGITATING
J. DISDAIN
K. MELANCHOLY
L. IMPAIRED
M. AVERTED
N. ASSENT
O. COVET
P. ALACRITY

1. A gradual rubbing away or wearing down
2. Turned away
3. Clever; inventive
4. Depressed; sad; gloomy
5. Contempt
6. Lower one's self to the position of inferiors
7. Eagerness
8. Ashamed; uneasy; disconcerted
9. Want
10. Painted
11. Thinking
12. Cautious
13. Fearless
14. Damaged; diminished in strength
15. Pale; dull; lifeless
16. Agreement

A=	B=	C=	D=
E=	F=	G=	H=
I=	J=	K=	L=
M=	N=	O=	P=

Tom Sawyer Vocabulary Magic Squares 1 Answer Key

Match the definition with the vocabulary word. Put your answers in the magic squares below. When your answers are correct, all columns and rows will add to the same number.

A. DAUNTLESS
B. INGENIOUS
C. CONDESCEND
D. WARY
E. ABASHED
F. FRESCOED
G. PALLID
H. ATTRITION
I. COGITATING
J. DISDAIN
K. MELANCHOLY
L. IMPAIRED
M. AVERTED
N. ASSENT
O. COVET
P. ALACRITY

1. A gradual rubbing away or wearing down
2. Turned away
3. Clever; inventive
4. Depressed; sad; gloomy
5. Contempt
6. Lower one's self to the position of inferiors
7. Eagerness
8. Ashamed; uneasy; disconcerted
9. Want
10. Painted
11. Thinking
12. Cautious
13. Fearless
14. Damaged; diminished in strength
15. Pale; dull; lifeless
16. Agreement

A=13	B=3	C=6	D=12
E=8	F=10	G=15	H=1
I=11	J=5	K=4	L=14
M=2	N=16	O=9	P=7

Tom Sawyer Vocabulary Magic Squares 2

Match the definition with the vocabulary word. Put your answers in the magic squares below. When your answers are correct, all columns and rows will add to the same number.

A. CONTRIVED
B. CARICATURE
C. DISDAIN
D. UPBRAID
E. INQUEST
F. PERPLEXED
G. COUNTENANCE
H. ABSTAIN
I. RESOLUTION
J. ATTRITION
K. CEASED
L. CHAOS
M. CONDESCEND
N. MELANCHOLY
O. SUBDUED
P. OPPRESSIVE

1. Drawing in which the subjects distinctive traits are exaggerated
2. Face
3. Stopped
4. Depressed; sad; gloomy
5. Lower one's self to the position of inferiors
6. Disorder; confusion
7. Stop doing something by one's own choice
8. Schemed
9. Difficult to bear
10. Determination
11. Judicial inquiry into the cause of a death
12. Reprimand
13. Contempt
14. Puzzled; uncertain
15. A gradual rubbing away or wearing down
16. Conquered and brought under control

A=	B=	C=	D=
E=	F=	G=	H=
I=	J=	K=	L=
M=	N=	O=	P=

Tom Sawyer Vocabulary Magic Squares 2 Answer Key

Match the definition with the vocabulary word. Put your answers in the magic squares below. When your answers are correct, all columns and rows will add to the same number.

A. CONTRIVED
B. CARICATURE
C. DISDAIN
D. UPBRAID
E. INQUEST
F. PERPLEXED
G. COUNTENANCE
H. ABSTAIN
I. RESOLUTION
J. ATTRITION
K. CEASED
L. CHAOS
M. CONDESCEND
N. MELANCHOLY
O. SUBDUED
P. OPPRESSIVE

1. Drawing in which the subjects distinctive traits are exaggerated
2. Face
3. Stopped
4. Depressed; sad; gloomy
5. Lower one's self to the position of inferiors
6. Disorder; confusion
7. Stop doing something by one's own choice
8. Schemed
9. Difficult to bear
10. Determination
11. Judicial inquiry into the cause of a death
12. Reprimand
13. Contempt
14. Puzzled; uncertain
15. A gradual rubbing away or wearing down
16. Conquered and brought under control

A=8	B=1	C=13	D=12
E=11	F=14	G=2	H=7
I=10	J=15	K=3	L=6
M=5	N=4	O=16	P=9

Tom Sawyer Vocabulary Magic Squares 3

Match the definition with the vocabulary word. Put your answers in the magic squares below. When your answers are correct, all columns and rows will add to the same number.

A. RESOLUTION
B. ODIOUS
C. CARICATURE
D. DERISION
E. UPBRAID
F. BLISS
G. CONTRIVED
H. WARY
I. UNPALATABLE
J. OPPRESSIVE
K. MUTUAL
L. INGENIOUS
M. AWED
N. CONSENT
O. CHAOS
P. ABASHED

1. Disorder; confusion
2. Ridicule
3. Difficult to bear
4. Reprimand
5. Unacceptable to the mind or senses
6. Extreme happiness
7. Ashamed; uneasy; disconcerted
8. Drawing in which the subjects distinctive traits are exaggerated
9. Cautious
10. Possessed in common
11. Determination
12. Agree to do something
13. Arousing a strong dislike or displeasure
14. Amazed with mixed emotions of reverence, respect, and dread
15. Schemed
16. Clever; inventive

A=	B=	C=	D=
E=	F=	G=	H=
I=	J=	K=	L=
M=	N=	O=	P=

Tom Sawyer Vocabulary Magic Squares 3 Answer Key

Match the definition with the vocabulary word. Put your answers in the magic squares below. When your answers are correct, all columns and rows will add to the same number.

A. RESOLUTION
B. ODIOUS
C. CARICATURE
D. DERISION
E. UPBRAID
F. BLISS
G. CONTRIVED
H. WARY
I. UNPALATABLE
J. OPPRESSIVE
K. MUTUAL
L. INGENIOUS
M. AWED
N. CONSENT
O. CHAOS
P. ABASHED

1. Disorder; confusion
2. Ridicule
3. Difficult to bear
4. Reprimand
5. Unacceptable to the mind or senses
6. Extreme happiness
7. Ashamed; uneasy; disconcerted
8. Drawing in which the subjects distinctive traits are exaggerated
9. Cautious
10. Possessed in common
11. Determination
12. Agree to do something
13. Arousing a strong dislike or displeasure
14. Amazed with mixed emotions of reverence, respect, and dread
15. Schemed
16. Clever; inventive

A=11	B=13	C=8	D=2
E=4	F=6	G=15	H=9
I=5	J=3	K=10	L=16
M=14	N=12	O=1	P=7

Tom Sawyer Vocabulary Magic Squares 4

Match the definition with the vocabulary word. Put your answers in the magic squares below. When your answers are correct, all columns and rows will add to the same number.

A. COVET
B. INVARIABLY
C. SMOTE
D. IMPERISHABLE
E. AWED
F. VICE
G. MELANCHOLY
H. SUPPLICATION
I. PRODIGIOUS
J. COGITATING
K. CARICATURE
L. UPBRAID
M. MUTUAL
N. OPPRESSIVE
O. RESOLUTION
P. ODIOUS

1. A plea
2. Want
3. Without change
4. Depressed; sad; gloomy
5. Thinking
6. Determination
7. Arousing a strong dislike or displeasure
8. Impressively great
9. Drawing in which the subjects distinctive traits are exaggerated
10. Difficult to bear
11. Possessed in common
12. Reprimand
13. Amazed with mixed emotions of reverence, respect, and dread
14. Indestructible
15. Inflicted a heavy blow upon
16. Bad habit

A=	B=	C=	D=
E=	F=	G=	H=
I=	J=	K=	L=
M=	N=	O=	P=

Tom Sawyer Vocabulary Magic Squares 4 Answer Key

Match the definition with the vocabulary word. Put your answers in the magic squares below. When your answers are correct, all columns and rows will add to the same number.

A. COVET
B. INVARIABLY
C. SMOTE
D. IMPERISHABLE
E. AWED
F. VICE
G. MELANCHOLY
H. SUPPLICATION
I. PRODIGIOUS
J. COGITATING
K. CARICATURE
L. UPBRAID
M. MUTUAL
N. OPPRESSIVE
O. RESOLUTION
P. ODIOUS

1. A plea
2. Want
3. Without change
4. Depressed; sad; gloomy
5. Thinking
6. Determination
7. Arousing a strong dislike or displeasure
8. Impressively great
9. Drawing in which the subjects distinctive traits are exaggerated
10. Difficult to bear
11. Possessed in common
12. Reprimand
13. Amazed with mixed emotions of reverence, respect, and dread
14. Indestructible
15. Inflicted a heavy blow upon
16. Bad habit

A=2	B=3	C=15	D=14
E=13	F=16	G=4	H=1
I=8	J=5	K=9	L=12
M=11	N=10	O=6	P=7

Tom Sawyer Vocabulary Word Search 1

Words are placed backwards, forward, diagonally, up and down. Clues listed below can help you find the words. Circle the hidden vocabulary words in the maze.

I	M	P	L	O	R	E	B	D	S	U	B	D	U	E	D	G	E	Z	K
M	Z	Q	D	E	S	A	E	P	P	A	I	I	P	D	P	S	L	X	Q
P	A	T	M	H	C	X	B	A	P	A	H	M	L	A	V	F	O	B	M
A	V	F	D	D	E	R	T	B	R	R	S	P	A	U	J	L	Q	A	W
I	E	P	B	L	E	T	K	B	Q	N	U	E	U	N	N	T	U	L	T
R	R	P	P	R	R	R	P	A	X	N	O	R	S	T	X	P	E	A	J
E	T	R	F	I	H	U	I	S	N	Y	M	I	I	L	M	E	N	C	J
D	E	V	T	J	S	M	S	S	M	N	I	S	B	E	N	R	T	R	Y
P	D	I	T	K	Q	M	A	E	I	M	N	H	L	S	O	V	E	I	S
Y	O	C	D	R	D	B	O	N	S	O	A	A	E	S	I	A	D	T	C
N	N	E	S	I	A	B	S	T	A	I	N	B	P	U	T	D	I	Y	N
B	W	L	L	S	L	O	S	S	E	C	G	L	R	N	U	I	O	L	G
A	R	L	H	D	A	E	L	U	H	S	A	E	E	P	L	N	U	B	J
C	A	E	C	H	U	K	N	O	S	K	M	S	C	A	O	G	S	A	V
P	D	G	C	Q	T	B	L	I	Z	F	N	S	I	L	S	T	D	I	B
V	S	G	N	K	U	Y	B	D	T	O	D	I	P	A	E	Y	I	R	M
A	E	I	M	C	M	Z	W	O	C	E	Q	L	I	T	R	R	S	A	K
I	A	N	S	M	O	Q	H	A	S	H	Y	B	C	A	J	A	D	V	L
N	R	Q	J	R	Q	V	L	A	R	M	J	G	E	B	G	N	A	N	C
C	O	N	D	E	S	C	E	N	D	Y	Q	B	F	L	P	N	I	I	D
W	H	C	A	R	I	C	A	T	U	R	E	K	N	E	W	Y	N	N	J

A gradual rubbing away or wearing down (9)
A ruler's unjust use of power (7)
Agree to do something (7)
Agreement (6)
Amazed with mixed emotions of reverence, respect, and dread (4)
Arousing a strong dislike or displeasure (6)
Ashamed; uneasy; disconcerted (7)
Bad habit (4)
Beg (7)
Believable (9)
Burn; scorch (4)
Calmed; satisfied; pacified (8)
Cautious (4)
Characterized by persuasive, powerful, or moving words (8)
Conquered and brought under control (7)
Contempt (7)
Courageously noble (11)
Damaged; diminished in strength (8)
Depressed; sad; gloomy (10)
Determination (10)
Disorder; confusion (5)
Drawing in which the subjects distinctive traits are exaggerated (10)
Eagerness (8)
Excessively proud (4)
Extreme happiness (5)
Fearless (9)
Indestructible (12)
Inflicted a heavy blow upon (5)
Judicial inquiry into the cause of a death (7)
Lower one's self to the position of inferiors (10)
Overhanging rock; cliff (9)
Pale; dull; lifeless (6)
Possessed in common (6)
Present throughout (9)
Puzzled; uncertain (9)
Reprimand (7)
Ridicule (8)
Stop doing something by one's own choice (7)
Stopped (6)
Tiresome by reason of extreme length or slowness (7)
Turned away (7)
Unacceptable to the mind or senses (11)
Want (5)
Without change (10)

Tom Sawyer Vocabulary Word Search 1 Answer Key

Words are placed backwards, forward, diagonally, up and down. Clues listed below can help you find the words. Circle the hidden vocabulary words in the maze.

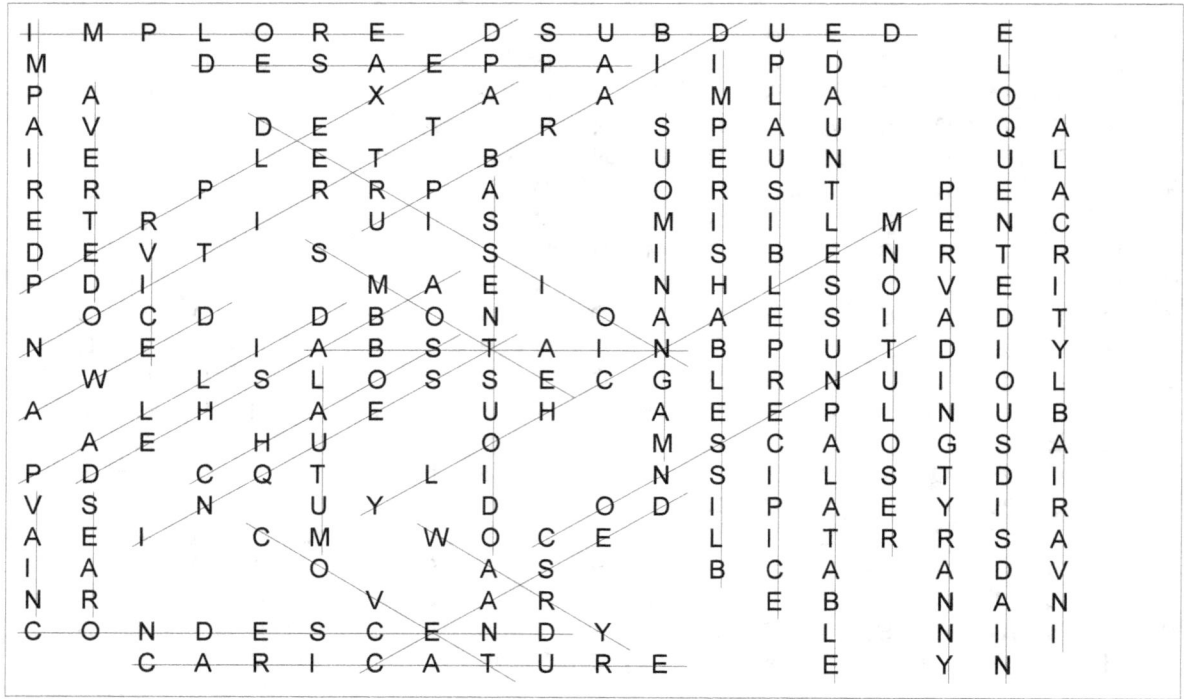

A gradual rubbing away or wearing down (9)
A ruler's unjust use of power (7)
Agree to do something (7)
Agreement (6)
Amazed with mixed emotions of reverence, respect, and dread (4)
Arousing a strong dislike or displeasure (6)
Ashamed; uneasy; disconcerted (7)
Bad habit (4)
Beg (7)
Believable (9)
Burn; scorch (4)
Calmed; satisfied; pacified (8)
Cautious (4)
Characterized by persuasive, powerful, or moving words (8)
Conquered and brought under control (7)
Contempt (7)
Courageously noble (11)
Damaged; diminished in strength (8)
Depressed; sad; gloomy (10)
Determination (10)
Disorder; confusion (5)
Drawing in which the subjects distinctive traits are exaggerated (10)
Eagerness (8)
Excessively proud (4)
Extreme happiness (5)
Fearless (9)
Indestructible (12)
Inflicted a heavy blow upon (5)
Judicial inquiry into the cause of a death (7)
Lower one's self to the position of inferiors (10)
Overhanging rock; cliff (9)
Pale; dull; lifeless (6)
Possessed in common (6)
Present throughout (9)
Puzzled; uncertain (9)
Reprimand (7)
Ridicule (8)
Stop doing something by one's own choice (7)
Stopped (6)
Tiresome by reason of extreme length or slowness (7)
Turned away (7)
Unacceptable to the mind or senses (11)
Want (5)
Without change (10)

Tom Sawyer Vocabulary Word Search 2

Words are placed backwards, forward, diagonally, up and down. Clues listed below can help you find the words. Circle the hidden vocabulary words in the maze.

```
P L A U S I B L E C N A N E T N U O C B
C R I F X P D F I A I T V C D B D T Y D
Y Y M R S R A Y M R A G N I D A V R E P
L F P E B O U U P I T B H P V P W D B T
H G L S D D N N A C S U O I R A C E R P
V N O C R I T P I A B F M C K L R V C X
S S R O X G L A R T A N G E F L G I H C
I U E E I I E L E U U P B R A I D R Z D
N T B D N O S A D R P C F P F D Z T S S
V H J D Q U S T R E S O L U T I O N U C
A R W D U S M A W F L N N Y T R I O P X
R Y E J E E B B P K C S O F A A I C P R
I W D G S E D L T H H E I E D D V W L V
A V E R T E D E I G G N S S O A H C I P
B L M O H Y V A L S V T I P I L T C C V
L C M S M O R B L O S D R N A A E D A Z
Y S E R C L W A R Y Q V E S S C D V T Q
X R T A H K U S N Q J U D P S R I X I B
K H H X S T C H H N T R E K E I O J O Q
M Z P M U E H E M M Y P J N N T U C N X
Q D M M M Y D D Y S F F P Y T Y S S Y H
```

A plea (12)
A ruler's unjust use of power (7)
Agree to do something (7)
Agreement (6)
Amazed with mixed emotions of reverence, respect, and dread (4)
Arousing a strong dislike or displeasure (6)
Ashamed; uneasy; disconcerted (7)
Bad habit (4)
Beg (7)
Believable (9)
Burn; scorch (4)
Cautious (4)
Characterized by persuasive, powerful, or moving words (8)
Conquered and brought under control (7)
Contempt (7)
Damaged; diminished in strength (8)
Dangerously lacking in security or stability (10)
Determination (10)
Disorder; confusion (5)
Drawing in which the subjects distinctive traits are exaggerated (10)
Eagerness (8)

Excessively proud (4)
Extreme happiness (5)
Face (11)
Fearless (9)
Impressively great (10)
Inflicted a heavy blow upon (5)
Judicial inquiry into the cause of a death (7)
Overhanging rock; cliff (9)
Painted (8)
Pale; dull; lifeless (6)
Possessed in common (6)
Present throughout (9)
Reprimand (7)
Ridicule (8)
Schemed (9)
Stop doing something by one's own choice (7)
Stopped (6)
Tiresome by reason of extreme length or slowness (7)
Turned away (7)
Unacceptable to the mind or senses (11)
Want (5)
Without change (10)

Tom Sawyer Vocabulary Word Search 2 Answer Key

Words are placed backwards, forward, diagonally, up and down. Clues listed below can help you find the words. Circle the hidden vocabulary words in the maze.

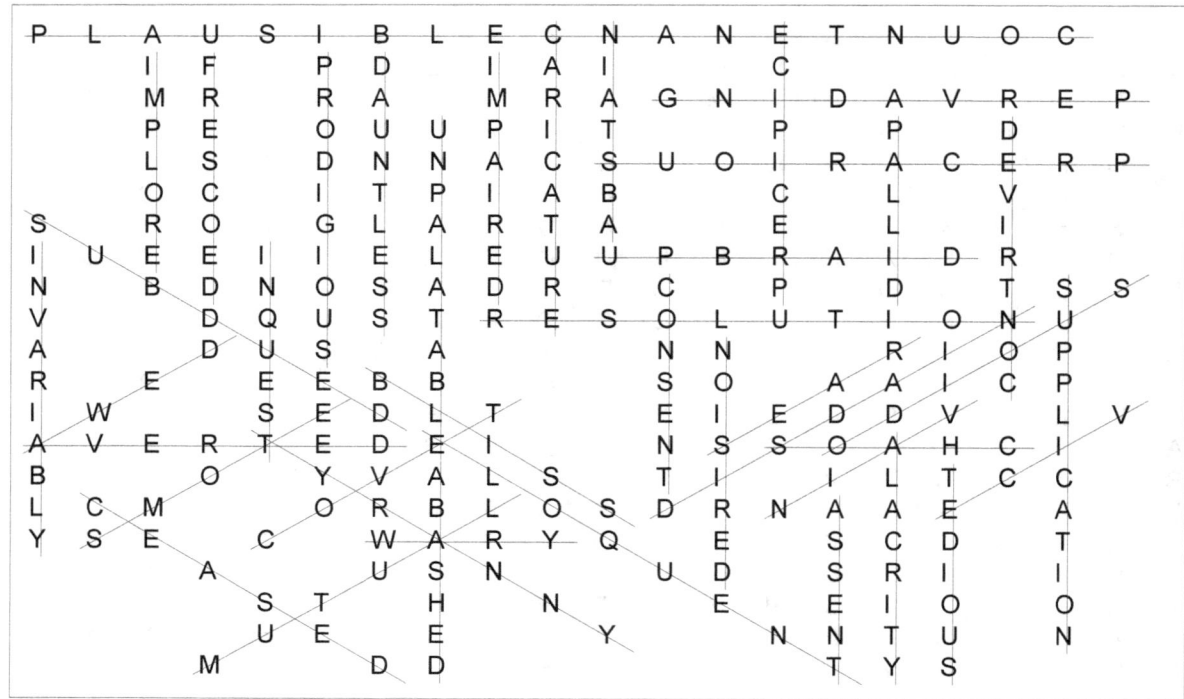

A plea (12)
A ruler's unjust use of power (7)
Agree to do something (7)
Agreement (6)
Amazed with mixed emotions of reverence, respect, and dread (4)
Arousing a strong dislike or displeasure (6)
Ashamed; uneasy; disconcerted (7)
Bad habit (4)
Beg (7)
Believable (9)
Burn; scorch (4)
Cautious (4)
Characterized by persuasive, powerful, or moving words (8)
Conquered and brought under control (7)
Contempt (7)
Damaged; diminished in strength (8)
Dangerously lacking in security or stability (10)
Determination (10)
Disorder; confusion (5)
Drawing in which the subjects distinctive traits are exaggerated (10)
Eagerness (8)

Excessively proud (4)
Extreme happiness (5)
Face (11)
Fearless (9)
Impressively great (10)
Inflicted a heavy blow upon (5)
Judicial inquiry into the cause of a death (7)
Overhanging rock; cliff (9)
Painted (8)
Pale; dull; lifeless (6)
Possessed in common (6)
Present throughout (9)
Reprimand (7)
Ridicule (8)
Schemed (9)
Stop doing something by one's own choice (7)
Stopped (6)
Tiresome by reason of extreme length or slowness (7)
Turned away (7)
Unacceptable to the mind or senses (11)
Want (5)
Without change (10)

Tom Sawyer Vocabulary Word Search 3

Words are placed backwards, forward, diagonally, up and down. Words listed below are included in the maze. Circle the hidden vocabulary words in the maze.

```
A P R E C A R I O U S D E R I S I O N G
B B E H L N Z V P U P E I E W L S B O R
S P A R J O Q P B G N S P S M P U L I W
T R G S P N Q D C I A A A O D L O I T C
A O H E H L U U A X V E L L E A M S I F
I D D C Y E E V E C E P L U V S I S R P
N I E I D M D X Z N R P I T I S N N T H
C G O P O W R A E S T A D I R E A C T Y
O I C I D U F C Z D E R V O T N N H A M
N O S C I F S O U D D C G N N T G A D J
D U E E A J Y N N A R Y T J O G A O S P
E S R R R G G S P D E S A E C Y M S E B
S W F P B V C E A H L L K T L G E V Z X
C V G M P R N N L S V W Q O K L I W P V
E I Z K U K N T A R Y B H G T S C B E J
N M L Z C T L J T S B C L N S O N A T Q
D P V Z N W U D A X N N U E V Q W S O R
T L T G T A B A B A H A R E C E V J M R
Y O Y T I R C A L A D P T E D I O U S K
Y R K K Z Y F E E T P C T T C V P S Q X
D E R I A P M I G O Z T S E U Q N I P R
```

ABASHED	CONDESCEND	INQUEST	RESOLUTION
ABSTAIN	CONSENT	MAGNANIMOUS	SEAR
ALACRITY	CONTRIVED	MELANCHOLY	SMOTE
APPEASED	COVET	MUTUAL	SUBDUED
ASSENT	DAUNTLESS	ODIOUS	TEDIOUS
ATTRITION	DERISION	OPPRESSIVE	TYRANNY
AVERTED	DISDAIN	PALLID	UNPALATABLE
AWED	ELOQUENT	PERPLEXED	UPBRAID
BLISS	FRESCOED	PRECARIOUS	VAIN
CEASED	IMPAIRED	PRECIPICE	VICE
CHAOS	IMPLORE	PRODIGIOUS	WARY

Tom Sawyer Vocabulary Word Search 3 Answer Key

Words are placed backwards, forward, diagonally, up and down. Words listed below are included in the maze. Circle the hidden vocabulary words in the maze.

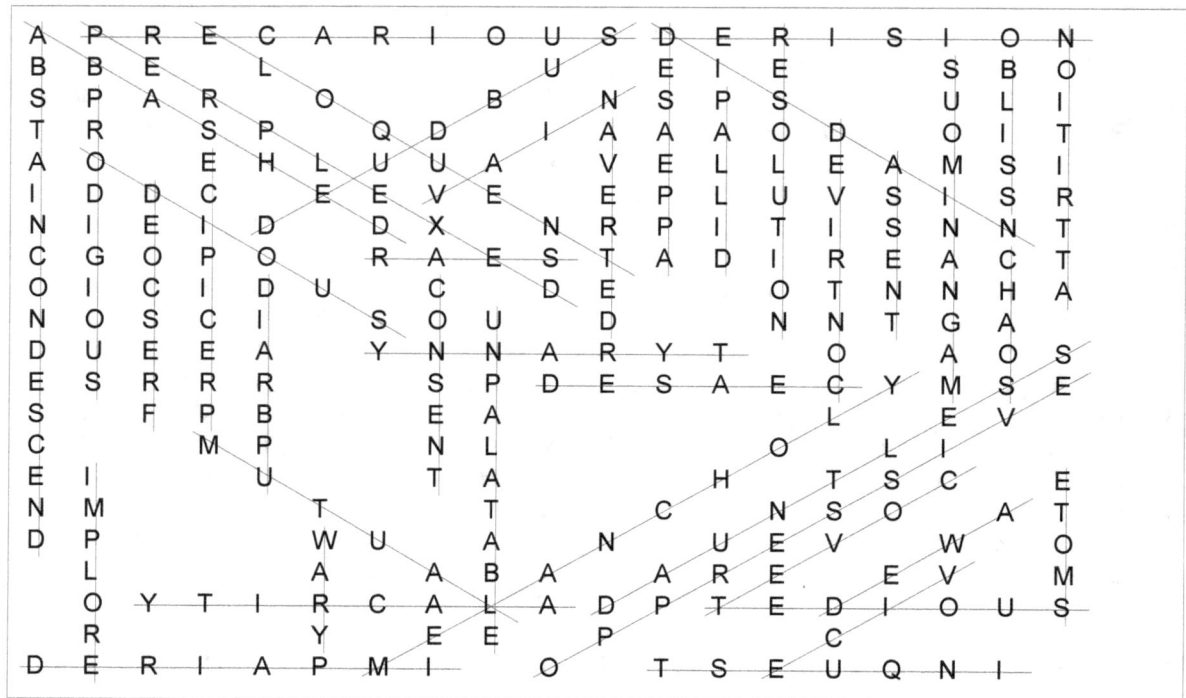

ABASHED	CONDESCEND	INQUEST	RESOLUTION
ABSTAIN	CONSENT	MAGNANIMOUS	SEAR
ALACRITY	CONTRIVED	MELANCHOLY	SMOTE
APPEASED	COVET	MUTUAL	SUBDUED
ASSENT	DAUNTLESS	ODIOUS	TEDIOUS
ATTRITION	DERISION	OPPRESSIVE	TYRANNY
AVERTED	DISDAIN	PALLID	UNPALATABLE
AWED	ELOQUENT	PERPLEXED	UPBRAID
BLISS	FRESCOED	PRECARIOUS	VAIN
CEASED	IMPAIRED	PRECIPICE	VICE
CHAOS	IMPLORE	PRODIGIOUS	WARY

Tom Sawyer Vocabulary Word Search 4

Words are placed backwards, forward, diagonally, up and down. Words listed below are included in the maze. Circle the hidden vocabulary words in the maze.

```
P A U N P A L A T A B L E O D I O U S P
R T E P W N H T O P P R E S S I V E L M
O T Y L B S C A L A C R I T Y B P P R R
D R N C O R C O G N I D A V R E P D E M
I I N R H Q A R U C N S L T R V N R U G
G T A Q R A U I M N G C I P F K O T E X
I I R E A M O E D N T R L M R L U Y C P
O O Y L E V I S N E H E R P P A L L I D
U N T B S L U U H T X S N M L A W T V F
S I F I R B J O M E P O I A B P I E H J
C A A S D R L M D N R L W D N Q Y R D F
O V V U T C C I T S E U Q N I C F D E G
N H E A E S A N S V C T K D A S E E C D
T D R L D N R A W S A I N E T H D S I J
R R T P I P I N A C R O X S S B E A P V
I T E V O C C G R O I N F A B W T E I J
V X D T U J A A Y N O W B E A N O P C N
E B N S S R T M J S U A M C E B M P E J
D G Z M V Y U Z H E S X D S X Y S A R S
N N O I S I R E D N E C S E D N O C P P
F R E S C O E D W T D A U N T L E S S X
```

ABASHED	CHAOS	IMPLORE	PRODIGIOUS
ABSTAIN	CONDESCEND	INQUEST	RESOLUTION
ALACRITY	CONSENT	MAGNANIMOUS	SEAR
APPEASED	CONTRIVED	MUTUAL	SMOTE
APPREHENSIVELY	COUNTENANCE	ODIOUS	SUBDUED
ASSENT	COVET	OPPRESSIVE	TEDIOUS
ATTRITION	DAUNTLESS	PALLID	TYRANNY
AVERTED	DERISION	PERPLEXED	UNPALATABLE
AWED	DISDAIN	PERVADING	UPBRAID
BLISS	ELOQUENT	PLAUSIBLE	VAIN
CARICATURE	FRESCOED	PRECARIOUS	VICE
CEASED	IMPAIRED	PRECIPICE	WARY

Tom Sawyer Vocabulary Word Search 4 Answer Key

Words are placed backwards, forward, diagonally, up and down. Words listed below are included in the maze. Circle the hidden vocabulary words in the maze.

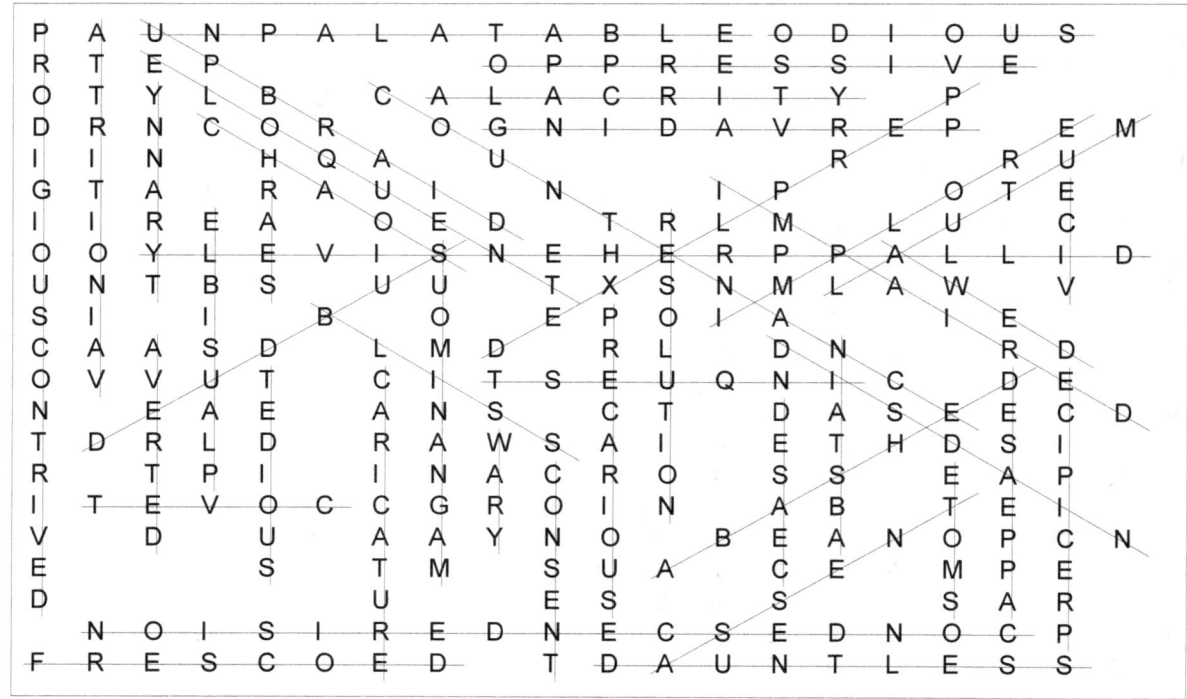

ABASHED	CHAOS	IMPLORE	PRODIGIOUS
ABSTAIN	CONDESCEND	INQUEST	RESOLUTION
ALACRITY	CONSENT	MAGNANIMOUS	SEAR
APPEASED	CONTRIVED	MUTUAL	SMOTE
APPREHENSIVELY	COUNTENANCE	ODIOUS	SUBDUED
ASSENT	COVET	OPPRESSIVE	TEDIOUS
ATTRITION	DAUNTLESS	PALLID	TYRANNY
AVERTED	DERISION	PERPLEXED	UNPALATABLE
AWED	DISDAIN	PERVADING	UPBRAID
BLISS	ELOQUENT	PLAUSIBLE	VAIN
CARICATURE	FRESCOED	PRECARIOUS	VICE
CEASED	IMPAIRED	PRECIPICE	WARY

Tom Sawyer Vocabulary Crossword 1

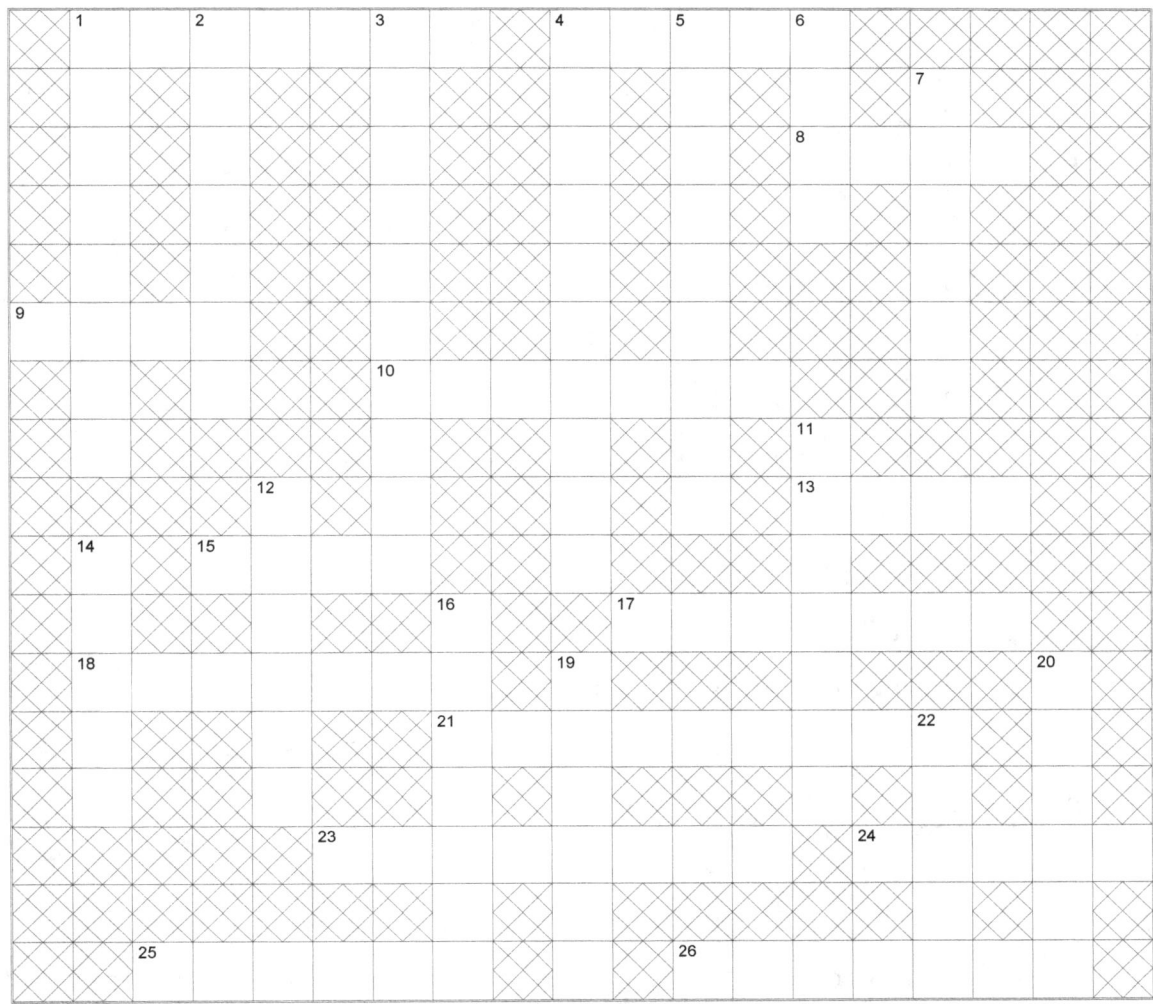

Across
1. Contempt
4. Disorder; confusion
8. Amazed with mixed emotions of reverence, respect, and dread
9. Bad habit
10. Stop doing something by one's own choice
13. Excessively proud
15. Cautious
17. Reprimand
18. Beg
21. Fearless
23. Characterized by persuasive, powerful, or moving words
24. Want
25. Arousing a strong dislike or displeasure
26. Agree to do something

Down
1. Ridicule
2. Conquered and brought under control
3. Without change
4. Drawing in which the subjects distinctive traits are exaggerated
5. A gradual rubbing away or wearing down
6. Burn; scorch
7. Stopped
11. Turned away
12. Pale; dull; lifeless
14. Extreme happiness
16. Tiresome by reason of extreme length or slowness
19. Possessed in common
20. Agreement
22. Inflicted a heavy blow upon

Tom Sawyer Vocabulary Crossword 1 Answer Key

Across
1. Contempt
4. Disorder; confusion
8. Amazed with mixed emotions of reverence, respect, and dread
9. Bad habit
10. Stop doing something by one's own choice
13. Excessively proud
15. Cautious
17. Reprimand
18. Beg
21. Fearless
23. Characterized by persuasive, powerful, or moving words
24. Want
25. Arousing a strong dislike or displeasure
26. Agree to do something

Down
1. Ridicule
2. Conquered and brought under control
3. Without change
4. Drawing in which the subjects distinctive traits are exaggerated
5. A gradual rubbing away or wearing down
6. Burn; scorch
7. Stopped
11. Turned away
12. Pale; dull; lifeless
14. Extreme happiness
16. Tiresome by reason of extreme length or slowness
19. Possessed in common
20. Agreement
22. Inflicted a heavy blow upon

Tom Sawyer Vocabulary Crossword 2

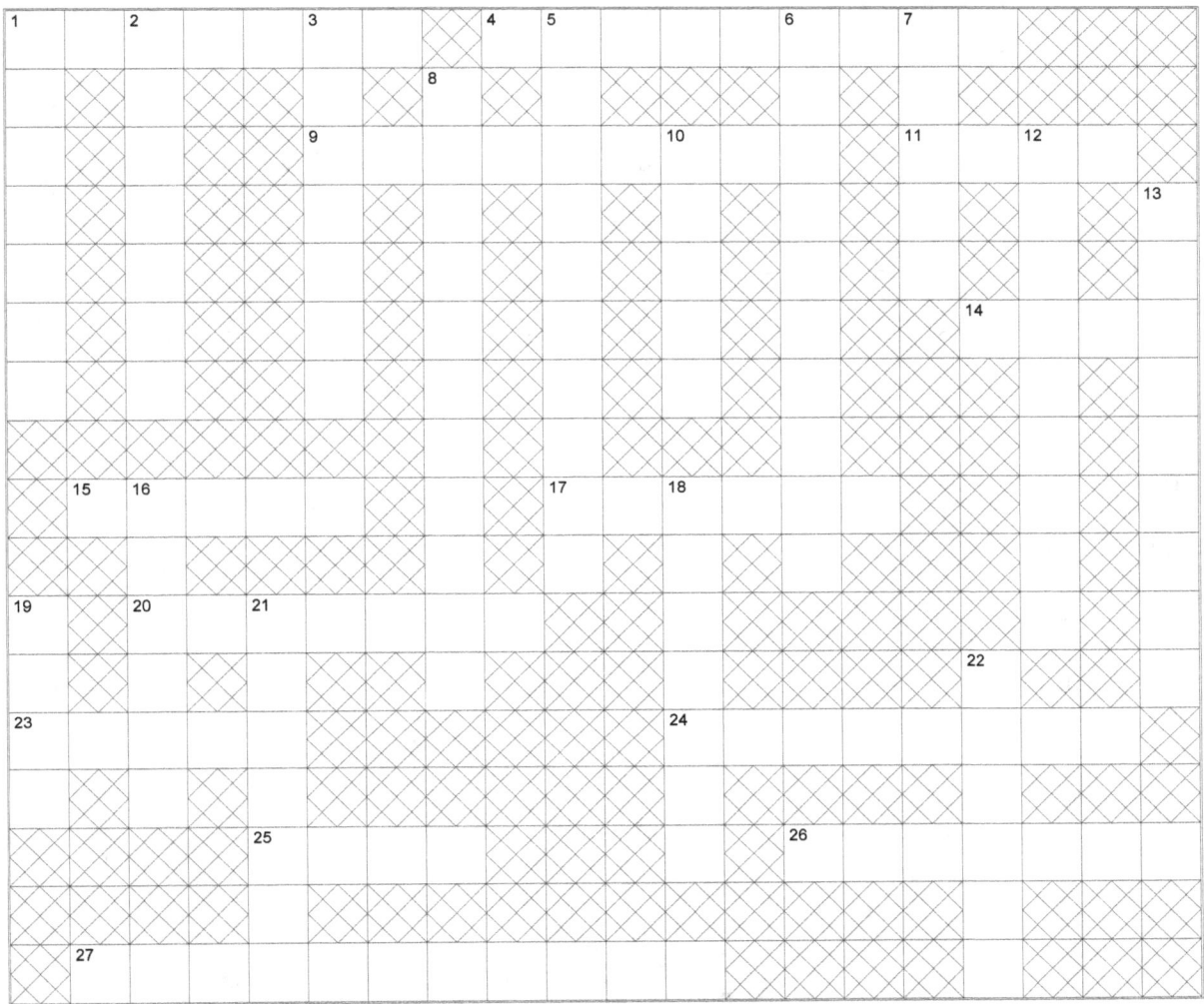

Across
1. Stop doing something by one's own choice
4. Overhanging rock; cliff
9. Believable
11. Excessively proud
14. Burn; scorch
15. Inflicted a heavy blow upon
17. Arousing a strong dislike or displeasure
20. Tiresome by reason of extreme length or slowness
23. Disorder; confusion
24. Characterized by persuasive, powerful, or moving words
25. Amazed with mixed emotions of reverence, respect, and dread
26. Agree to do something
27. Face

Down
1. Turned away
2. Conquered and brought under control
3. Beg
5. Determination
6. Dangerously lacking in security or stability
7. Want
8. Courageously noble
10. Extreme happiness
12. Clever; inventive
13. Puzzled; uncertain
16. Possessed in common
18. Judicial inquiry into the cause of a death
19. Bad habit
21. Contempt
22. Stopped

Tom Sawyer Vocabulary Crossword 2 Answer Key

Across
1. Stop doing something by one's own choice
4. Overhanging rock; cliff
9. Believable
11. Excessively proud
14. Burn; scorch
15. Inflicted a heavy blow upon
17. Arousing a strong dislike or displeasure
20. Tiresome by reason of extreme length or slowness
23. Disorder; confusion
24. Characterized by persuasive, powerful, or moving words
25. Amazed with mixed emotions of reverence, respect, and dread
26. Agree to do something
27. Face

Down
1. Turned away
2. Conquered and brought under control
3. Beg
5. Determination
6. Dangerously lacking in security or stability
7. Want
8. Courageously noble
10. Extreme happiness
12. Clever; inventive
13. Puzzled; uncertain
16. Possessed in common
18. Judicial inquiry into the cause of a death
19. Bad habit
21. Contempt
22. Stopped

Tom Sawyer Vocabulary Crossword 3

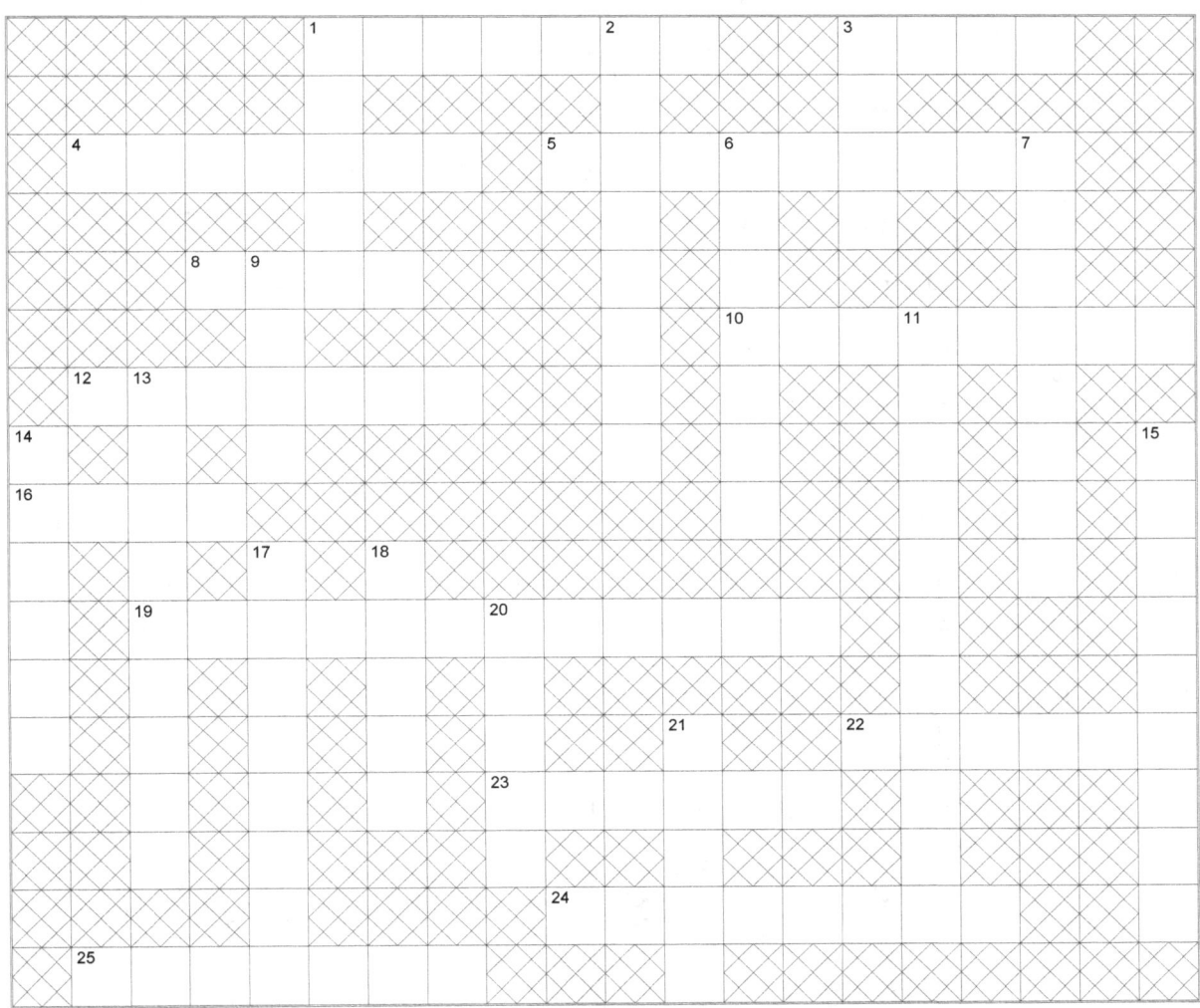

Across
1. Conquered and brought under control
3. Bad habit
4. Tiresome by reason of extreme length or slowness
5. Schemed
8. Amazed with mixed emotions of reverence, respect, and dread
10. Eagerness
12. Reprimand
16. Burn; scorch
19. A plea
22. Pale; dull; lifeless
23. Arousing a strong dislike or displeasure
24. Painted
25. Contempt

Down
1. Inflicted a heavy blow upon
2. Characterized by persuasive, powerful, or moving words
3. Excessively proud
6. A ruler's unjust use of power
7. Ridicule
9. Cautious
11. Face
13. Believable
14. Agreement
15. Present throughout
17. Calmed; satisfied; pacified
18. Extreme happiness
20. Disorder; confusion
21. Want

Tom Sawyer Vocabulary Crossword 3 Answer Key

Across
1. Conquered and brought under control
3. Bad habit
4. Tiresome by reason of extreme length or slowness
5. Schemed
8. Amazed with mixed emotions of reverence, respect, and dread
10. Eagerness
12. Reprimand
16. Burn; scorch
19. A plea
22. Pale; dull; lifeless
23. Arousing a strong dislike or displeasure
24. Painted
25. Contempt

Down
1. Inflicted a heavy blow upon
2. Characterized by persuasive, powerful, or moving words
3. Excessively proud
6. A ruler's unjust use of power
7. Ridicule
9. Cautious
11. Face
13. Believable
14. Agreement
15. Present throughout
17. Calmed; satisfied; pacified
18. Extreme happiness
20. Disorder; confusion
21. Want

Tom Sawyer Vocabulary Crossword 4

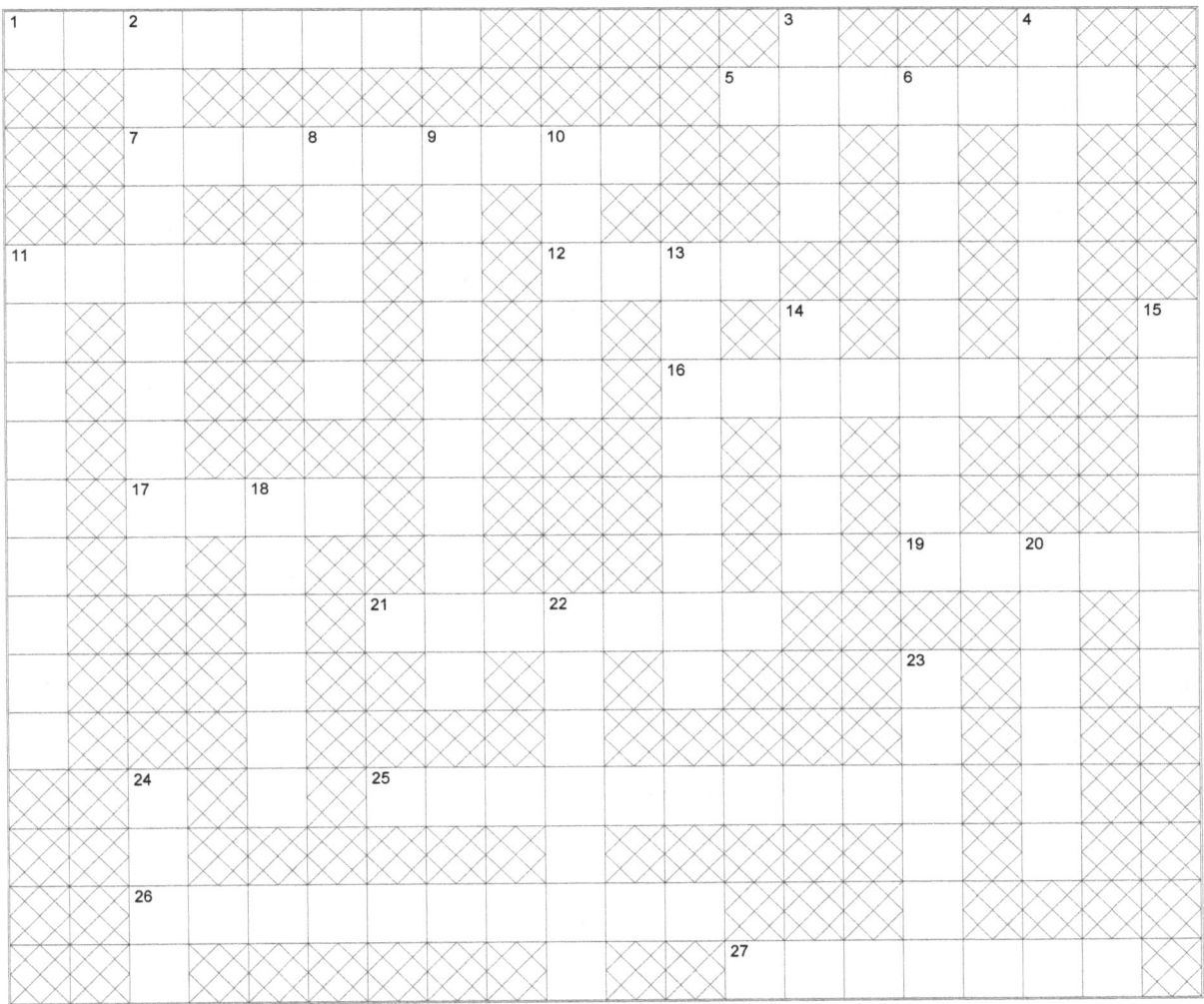

Across
1. Characterized by persuasive, powerful, or moving words
5. Tiresome by reason of extreme length or slowness
7. Overhanging rock; cliff
11. Amazed with mixed emotions of reverence, respect, and dread
12. Excessively proud
16. Pale; dull; lifeless
17. Bad habit
19. Inflicted a heavy blow upon
21. Conquered and brought under control
25. Impressively great
26. Determination
27. Stop doing something by one's own choice

Down
2. Difficult to bear
3. Burn; scorch
4. Possessed in common
6. Clever; inventive
8. Disorder; confusion
9. Dangerously lacking in security or stability
10. Want
11. A gradual rubbing away or wearing down
13. Damaged; diminished in strength
14. Extreme happiness
15. Judicial inquiry into the cause of a death
18. Stopped
20. Arousing a strong dislike or displeasure
22. Contempt
23. Agreement
24. Cautious

Tom Sawyer Vocabulary Crossword 4 Answer Key

	1	2									3			4	
	E	L	O	Q	U	E	N	T			S			M	
		P								5			6		
		P								T	E	D	I	O	U	S
		7		8		9		10							
		P	R	E	C	I	P	I	C	E		A		N	T
		R		H		R		O				R		G	U
	11									12	13				
	A	W	E	D		A		E		V	A	I	N	E	A
	T		S			O		C		E		M	14	N	L	15
	T		S			S		A		T		16	B		L	I
	T		S			S		A		T		P	A	L	L	I	D		N
	R		I					R				A		I		O		Q
		17		18											
	I	V	I	C	E			I				I		S		U		U
		E		E				O				R		S	19	S	M	O	T	E	20
				21			22								
	I			A		S	U	B	D	U	E	D				D		S
	O			S			S		I		D		23	A		I		T
	N			E					S					S		O	
		24				25									
		W		D		P	R	O	D	I	G	I	O	U	S	
		A							A					E	S	
		26													
		R	E	S	O	L	U	T	I	O	N			N	
		Y						N		27	A	B	S	T	A	I	N

Across
1. Characterized by persuasive, powerful, or moving words
5. Tiresome by reason of extreme length or slowness
7. Overhanging rock; cliff
11. Amazed with mixed emotions of reverence, respect, and dread
12. Excessively proud
16. Pale; dull; lifeless
17. Bad habit
19. Inflicted a heavy blow upon
21. Conquered and brought under control
25. Impressively great
26. Determination
27. Stop doing something by one's own choice

Down
2. Difficult to bear
3. Burn; scorch
4. Possessed in common
6. Clever; inventive
8. Disorder; confusion
9. Dangerously lacking in security or stability
10. Want
11. A gradual rubbing away or wearing down
13. Damaged; diminished in strength
14. Extreme happiness
15. Judicial inquiry into the cause of a death
18. Stopped
20. Arousing a strong dislike or displeasure
22. Contempt
23. Agreement
24. Cautious

Tom Sawyer Vocabulary Juggle Letters 1

1. LSSDUTANE = 1. _____
   Fearless

2. DSECEA = 2. _____
   Stopped

3. LPPIAITONUSC = 3. _____
   A plea

4. ISRUIDOGOP = 4. _____
   Impressively great

5. TNGOIICAGT = 5. _____
   Thinking

6. CEVTO = 6. _____
   Want

7. AHSIMPELIEBR = 7. _____
   Indestructible

8. RCCEPPEII = 8. _____
   Overhanging rock; cliff

9. YNRANYT = 9. _____
   A ruler's unjust use of power

10. IPDALL =10. _____
    Pale; dull; lifeless

11. TATITIORN =11. _____
    A gradual rubbing away or wearing down

12. XDRPEPLEE =12. _____
    Puzzled; uncertain

13. YLNOCMLHEA =13. _____
    Depressed; sad; gloomy

14. AIARBVYLIN =14. _____
    Without change

15. LATUMU =15. _____
    Possessed in common

Tom Sawyer Vocabulary Juggle Letters 1 Answer Key

1. LSSDUTANE = 1. DAUNTLESS
Fearless

2. DSECEA = 2. CEASED
Stopped

3. LPPIAITONUSC = 3. SUPPLICATION
A plea

4. ISRUIDOGOP = 4. PRODIGIOUS
Impressively great

5. TNGOIICAGT = 5. COGITATING
Thinking

6. CEVTO = 6. COVET
Want

7. AHSIMPELIEBR = 7. IMPERISHABLE
Indestructible

8. RCCEPPEII = 8. PRECIPICE
Overhanging rock; cliff

9. YNRANYT = 9. TYRANNY
A ruler's unjust use of power

10. IPDALL = 10. PALLID
Pale; dull; lifeless

11. TATITIORN = 11. ATTRITION
A gradual rubbing away or wearing down

12. XDRPEPLEE = 12. PERPLEXED
Puzzled; uncertain

13. YLNOCMLHEA = 13. MELANCHOLY
Depressed; sad; gloomy

14. AIARBVYLIN = 14. INVARIABLY
Without change

15. LATUMU = 15. MUTUAL
Possessed in common

Tom Sawyer Vocabulary Juggle Letters 2

1. WDAE = 1. _____
Amazed with mixed emotions of reverence, respect, and dread

2. NVAI = 2. _____
Excessively proud

3. SITNABA = 3. _____
Stop doing something by one's own choice

4. ISOIPDRUOG = 4. _____
Impressively great

5. ETRVAED = 5. _____
Turned away

6. TOECENNUCAN = 6. _____
Face

7. DACEES = 7. _____
Stopped

8. DBUIARP = 8. _____
Reprimand

9. PELEDERPX = 9. _____
Puzzled; uncertain

10. INSAUOMNMGA =10. _____
Courageously noble

11. ENQITUS =11. _____
Judicial inquiry into the cause of a death

12. DEUBUSD =12. _____
Conquered and brought under control

13. ENTSAS =13. _____
Agreement

14. ABYILNRAIV =14. _____
Without change

15. LUTONEQE =15. _____
Characterized by persuasive, powerful, or moving words

Tom Sawyer Vocabulary Juggle Letters 2 Answer Key

1. WDAE = 1. AWED
   Amazed with mixed emotions of reverence, respect, and dread
2. NVAI = 2. VAIN
   Excessively proud
3. SITNABA = 3. ABSTAIN
   Stop doing something by one's own choice
4. ISOIPDRUOG = 4. PRODIGIOUS
   Impressively great
5. ETRVAED = 5. AVERTED
   Turned away
6. TOECENNUCAN = 6. COUNTENANCE
   Face
7. DACEES = 7. CEASED
   Stopped
8. DBUIARP = 8. UPBRAID
   Reprimand
9. PELEDERPX = 9. PERPLEXED
   Puzzled; uncertain
10. INSAUOMNMGA = 10. MAGNANIMOUS
    Courageously noble
11. ENQITUS = 11. INQUEST
    Judicial inquiry into the cause of a death
12. DEUBUSD = 12. SUBDUED
    Conquered and brought under control
13. ENTSAS = 13. ASSENT
    Agreement
14. ABYILNRAIV = 14. INVARIABLY
    Without change
15. LUTONEQE = 15. ELOQUENT
    Characterized by persuasive, powerful, or moving words

Tom Sawyer Vocabulary Juggle Letters 3

1. SICEPAORUR = 1. _____
Dangerously lacking in security or stability

2. PREPIICCE = 2. _____
Overhanging rock; cliff

3. ARES = 3. _____
Burn; scorch

4. SOOUDI = 4. _____
Arousing a strong dislike or displeasure

5. PPCULSONITIA = 5. _____
A plea

6. SLISB = 6. _____
Extreme happiness

7. TECOV = 7. _____
Want

8. ENSUQIT = 8. _____
Judicial inquiry into the cause of a death

9. IANV = 9. _____
Excessively proud

10. VRAEDET =10. _____
Turned away

11. QTEUOENL =11. _____
Characterized by persuasive, powerful, or moving words

12. EPPEERXLD =12. _____
Puzzled; uncertain

13. AMULUT =13. _____
Possessed in common

14. ORISIOUPDG =14. _____
Impressively great

15. IPDLLA =15. _____
Pale; dull; lifeless

Tom Sawyer Vocabulary Juggle Letters 3 Answer Key

1. SICEPAORUR = 1. PRECARIOUS
   Dangerously lacking in security or stability

2. PREPIICCE = 2. PRECIPICE
   Overhanging rock; cliff

3. ARES = 3. SEAR
   Burn; scorch

4. SOOUDI = 4. ODIOUS
   Arousing a strong dislike or displeasure

5. PPCULSONITIA = 5. SUPPLICATION
   A plea

6. SLISB = 6. BLISS
   Extreme happiness

7. TECOV = 7. COVET
   Want

8. ENSUQIT = 8. INQUEST
   Judicial inquiry into the cause of a death

9. IANV = 9. VAIN
   Excessively proud

10. VRAEDET =10. AVERTED
    Turned away

11. QTEUOENL =11. ELOQUENT
    Characterized by persuasive, powerful, or moving words

12. EPPEERXLD =12. PERPLEXED
    Puzzled; uncertain

13. AMULUT =13. MUTUAL
    Possessed in common

14. ORISIOUPDG =14. PRODIGIOUS
    Impressively great

15. IPDLLA =15. PALLID
    Pale; dull; lifeless

Tom Sawyer Vocabulary Juggle Letters 4

1. ITGIGONTAC = 1. _____
   Thinking

2. UDUESBD = 2. _____
   Conquered and brought under control

3. EASPRCORUI = 3. _____
   Dangerously lacking in security or stability

4. EATVERD = 4. _____
   Turned away

5. EVCI = 5. _____
   Bad habit

6. IVNERDAPG = 6. _____
   Present throughout

7. DWAE = 7. _____
   Amazed with mixed emotions of reverence, respect, and dread

8. PEDPAAES = 8. _____
   Calmed; satisfied; pacified

9. SEUTDIO = 9. _____
   Tiresome by reason of extreme length or slowness

10. DOSCREFE = 10. _____
    Painted

11. AIPDUBR = 11. _____
    Reprimand

12. ABTSAIN = 12. _____
    Stop doing something by one's own choice

13. TINTTRAIO = 13. _____
    A gradual rubbing away or wearing down

14. HSOCA = 14. _____
    Disorder; confusion

15. CEEIICPRP = 15. _____
    Overhanging rock; cliff

Tom Sawyer Vocabulary Juggle Letters 4 Answer Key

1. ITGIGONTAC = 1. COGITATING
Thinking

2. UDUESBD = 2. SUBDUED
Conquered and brought under control

3. EASPRCORUI = 3. PRECARIOUS
Dangerously lacking in security or stability

4. EATVERD = 4. AVERTED
Turned away

5. EVCI = 5. VICE
Bad habit

6. IVNERDAPG = 6. PERVADING
Present throughout

7. DWAE = 7. AWED
Amazed with mixed emotions of reverence, respect, and dread

8. PEDPAAES = 8. APPEASED
Calmed; satisfied; pacified

9. SEUTDIO = 9. TEDIOUS
Tiresome by reason of extreme length or slowness

10. DOSCREFE = 10. FRESCOED
Painted

11. AIPDUBR = 11. UPBRAID
Reprimand

12. ABTSAIN = 12. ABSTAIN
Stop doing something by one's own choice

13. TINTTRAIO = 13. ATTRITION
A gradual rubbing away or wearing down

14. HSOCA = 14. CHAOS
Disorder; confusion

15. CEEIICPRP = 15. PRECIPICE
Overhanging rock; cliff

ABASHED	Ashamed; uneasy; disconcerted
ABSTAIN	Stop doing something by one's own choice
ALACRITY	Eagerness
APPEASED	Calmed; satisfied; pacified
APPREHENSIVELY	Anxiously; with reservation
ASSENT	Agreement
ATTRITION	A gradual rubbing away or wearing down

AVERTED	Turned away
AWED	Amazed with mixed emotions of reverence, respect, and dread
BLISS	Extreme happiness
CARICATURE	Drawing in which the subjects distinctive traits are exaggerated
CEASED	Stopped
CHAOS	Disorder; confusion
COGITATING	Thinking

CONDESCEND	Lower one's self to the position of inferiors
CONSENT	Agree to do something
CONTRIVED	Schemed
COUNTENANCE	Face
COVET	Want
DAUNTLESS	Fearless
DERISION	Ridicule

DISDAIN	Contempt
ELOQUENT	Characterized by persuasive, powerful, or moving words
FRESCOED	Painted
IMPAIRED	Damaged; diminished in strength
IMPERISHABLE	Indestructible
IMPLORE	Beg
INGENIOUS	Clever; inventive

INQUEST	Judicial inquiry into the cause of a death
INVARIABLY	Without change
MAGNANIMOUS	Courageously noble
MELANCHOLY	Depressed; sad; gloomy
MUTUAL	Possessed in common
ODIOUS	Arousing a strong dislike or displeasure
OPPRESSIVE	Difficult to bear

PALLID	Pale; dull; lifeless
PERPLEXED	Puzzled; uncertain
PERVADING	Present throughout
PLAUSIBLE	Believable
PRECARIOUS	Dangerously lacking in security or stability
PRECIPICE	Overhanging rock; cliff
PRODIGIOUS	Impressively great

RESOLUTION	Determination
SEAR	Burn; scorch
SMOTE	Inflicted a heavy blow upon
SUBDUED	Conquered and brought under control
SUPPLICATION	A plea
TEDIOUS	Tiresome by reason of extreme length or slowness
TYRANNY	A ruler's unjust use of power

UNPALATABLE	Unacceptable to the mind or senses
UPBRAID	Reprimand
VAIN	Excessively proud
VICE	Bad habit
WARY	Cautious

Tom Sawyer Vocabulary

APPREHENSIVELY	APPEASED	DAUNTLESS	CARICATURE	RESOLUTION
CEASED	IMPERISHABLE	SMOTE	MELANCHOLY	ELOQUENT
VAIN	DERISION	FREE SPACE	SUBDUED	VICE
SUPPLICATION	ALACRITY	MAGNANIMOUS	IMPAIRED	COUNTENANCE
ABSTAIN	PLAUSIBLE	CONTRIVED	PERPLEXED	ABASHED

Tom Sawyer Vocabulary

CONSENT	INGENIOUS	OPPRESSIVE	MUTUAL	FRESCOED
AWED	COGITATING	IMPLORE	INQUEST	DISDAIN
CONDESCEND	WARY	FREE SPACE	TEDIOUS	SEAR
PERVADING	PRODIGIOUS	COVET	PRECIPICE	ASSENT
ATTRITION	UNPALATABLE	UPBRAID	TYRANNY	ODIOUS

Tom Sawyer Vocabulary

MUTUAL	IMPERISHABLE	BLISS	PERVADING	ELOQUENT
INVARIABLY	ATTRITION	TEDIOUS	ASSENT	CHAOS
CONSENT	CONDESCEND	FREE SPACE	ABASHED	SUPPLICATION
UNPALATABLE	DAUNTLESS	APPREHENSIVELY	TYRANNY	APPEASED
IMPAIRED	ABSTAIN	CONTRIVED	PLAUSIBLE	COUNTENANCE

Tom Sawyer Vocabulary

INGENIOUS	CARICATURE	UPBRAID	VAIN	PRODIGIOUS
CEASED	SUBDUED	DISDAIN	PERPLEXED	RESOLUTION
PRECARIOUS	SEAR	FREE SPACE	AWED	MELANCHOLY
SMOTE	INQUEST	AVERTED	COGITATING	PRECIPICE
WARY	DERISION	ODIOUS	PALLID	IMPLORE

Tom Sawyer Vocabulary

TEDIOUS	MUTUAL	ATTRITION	CONSENT	COGITATING
VAIN	PRECARIOUS	CEASED	COUNTENANCE	ODIOUS
SEAR	PERPLEXED	FREE SPACE	ALACRITY	CONTRIVED
UNPALATABLE	SUPPLICATION	IMPLORE	INGENIOUS	ABASHED
APPEASED	DERISION	PALLID	PERVADING	PLAUSIBLE

Tom Sawyer Vocabulary

INQUEST	IMPAIRED	MELANCHOLY	ASSENT	AWED
ELOQUENT	FRESCOED	DAUNTLESS	PRECIPICE	OPPRESSIVE
APPREHENSIVELY	SMOTE	FREE SPACE	WARY	RESOLUTION
MAGNANIMOUS	DISDAIN	CARICATURE	PRODIGIOUS	IMPERISHABLE
AVERTED	COVET	VICE	ABSTAIN	BLISS

Tom Sawyer Vocabulary

PERVADING	ASSENT	PALLID	DERISION	PRODIGIOUS
CARICATURE	VAIN	AVERTED	SUBDUED	RESOLUTION
IMPAIRED	UNPALATABLE	FREE SPACE	AWED	COVET
COUNTENANCE	IMPLORE	UPBRAID	ODIOUS	CEASED
SMOTE	CONTRIVED	TEDIOUS	DAUNTLESS	COGITATING

Tom Sawyer Vocabulary

MELANCHOLY	MAGNANIMOUS	SEAR	INQUEST	CONSENT
BLISS	ATTRITION	ABASHED	APPEASED	DISDAIN
PERPLEXED	IMPERISHABLE	FREE SPACE	TYRANNY	PRECARIOUS
ALACRITY	WARY	OPPRESSIVE	INVARIABLY	PRECIPICE
SUPPLICATION	ELOQUENT	PLAUSIBLE	FRESCOED	CHAOS

Tom Sawyer Vocabulary

DERISION	IMPLORE	CONDESCEND	WARY	PRECARIOUS
INGENIOUS	OPPRESSIVE	PRODIGIOUS	ODIOUS	ABSTAIN
CONSENT	DISDAIN	FREE SPACE	IMPERISHABLE	SMOTE
SUPPLICATION	PRECIPICE	ALACRITY	MELANCHOLY	UPBRAID
UNPALATABLE	APPREHENSIVELY	INVARIABLY	DAUNTLESS	COVET

Tom Sawyer Vocabulary

MUTUAL	PERPLEXED	SUBDUED	FRESCOED	MAGNANIMOUS
ASSENT	CARICATURE	VICE	SEAR	CHAOS
APPEASED	CONTRIVED	FREE SPACE	PERVADING	AWED
BLISS	TYRANNY	VAIN	CEASED	COUNTENANCE
INQUEST	COGITATING	AVERTED	TEDIOUS	IMPAIRED

Tom Sawyer Vocabulary

IMPAIRED	OPPRESSIVE	COUNTENANCE	ABSTAIN	COVET
PERVADING	SMOTE	UNPALATABLE	IMPERISHABLE	INGENIOUS
PERPLEXED	RESOLUTION	FREE SPACE	FRESCOED	UPBRAID
CONSENT	SEAR	APPREHENSIVELY	PRODIGIOUS	AWED
TEDIOUS	TYRANNY	VAIN	CONDESCEND	MAGNANIMOUS

Tom Sawyer Vocabulary

COGITATING	DAUNTLESS	ABASHED	IMPLORE	VICE
SUBDUED	DERISION	MUTUAL	SUPPLICATION	ELOQUENT
WARY	INVARIABLY	FREE SPACE	CEASED	PRECIPICE
PALLID	APPEASED	CARICATURE	INQUEST	PLAUSIBLE
ALACRITY	CHAOS	AVERTED	ASSENT	DISDAIN

Tom Sawyer Vocabulary

CEASED	OPPRESSIVE	CONDESCEND	AVERTED	UNPALATABLE
APPREHENSIVELY	ATTRITION	IMPERISHABLE	TEDIOUS	DISDAIN
FRESCOED	COGITATING	FREE SPACE	CHAOS	MELANCHOLY
CONTRIVED	INGENIOUS	UPBRAID	PERPLEXED	MAGNANIMOUS
PRECARIOUS	SMOTE	ODIOUS	SUPPLICATION	ABSTAIN

Tom Sawyer Vocabulary

SEAR	APPEASED	VICE	TYRANNY	PERVADING
CARICATURE	AWED	INVARIABLY	WARY	ELOQUENT
MUTUAL	CONSENT	FREE SPACE	BLISS	INQUEST
PALLID	ASSENT	DERISION	COUNTENANCE	IMPAIRED
IMPLORE	RESOLUTION	ALACRITY	COVET	PRODIGIOUS

Tom Sawyer Vocabulary

ODIOUS	DERISION	APPEASED	CEASED	CARICATURE
IMPAIRED	PRECARIOUS	DAUNTLESS	SUPPLICATION	PERVADING
ASSENT	COVET	FREE SPACE	VAIN	SUBDUED
ALACRITY	IMPERISHABLE	OPPRESSIVE	PLAUSIBLE	CHAOS
INVARIABLY	CONDESCEND	MUTUAL	PRODIGIOUS	SEAR

Tom Sawyer Vocabulary

DISDAIN	APPREHENSIVELY	INGENIOUS	FRESCOED	UNPALATABLE
PERPLEXED	TEDIOUS	VICE	AWED	RESOLUTION
IMPLORE	CONSENT	FREE SPACE	COGITATING	MELANCHOLY
SMOTE	INQUEST	COUNTENANCE	ABASHED	AVERTED
WARY	PRECIPICE	ATTRITION	UPBRAID	ELOQUENT

Tom Sawyer Vocabulary

UNPALATABLE	ALACRITY	UPBRAID	IMPERISHABLE	TEDIOUS
PLAUSIBLE	AVERTED	MUTUAL	DERISION	OPPRESSIVE
CONDESCEND	CONSENT	FREE SPACE	ODIOUS	PERPLEXED
PRODIGIOUS	MAGNANIMOUS	PERVADING	ABSTAIN	MELANCHOLY
VAIN	AWED	APPEASED	COVET	INQUEST

Tom Sawyer Vocabulary

VICE	DAUNTLESS	ABASHED	BLISS	FRESCOED
SUPPLICATION	ELOQUENT	CONTRIVED	PRECARIOUS	CHAOS
INGENIOUS	COGITATING	FREE SPACE	PALLID	PRECIPICE
TYRANNY	IMPAIRED	ASSENT	CARICATURE	RESOLUTION
SEAR	ATTRITION	WARY	INVARIABLY	COUNTENANCE

Tom Sawyer Vocabulary

MAGNANIMOUS	APPEASED	AWED	DAUNTLESS	CEASED
PRECIPICE	MUTUAL	FRESCOED	COGITATING	BLISS
IMPERISHABLE	TEDIOUS	FREE SPACE	IMPLORE	MELANCHOLY
UNPALATABLE	PALLID	AVERTED	COUNTENANCE	CHAOS
INVARIABLY	RESOLUTION	PRODIGIOUS	ASSENT	DISDAIN

Tom Sawyer Vocabulary

COVET	INQUEST	SUPPLICATION	INGENIOUS	IMPAIRED
PRECARIOUS	ABSTAIN	TYRANNY	PERVADING	SMOTE
CONTRIVED	DERISION	FREE SPACE	WARY	UPBRAID
SEAR	ABASHED	VAIN	ELOQUENT	ALACRITY
CONDESCEND	APPREHENSIVELY	VICE	SUBDUED	CONSENT

Tom Sawyer Vocabulary

FRESCOED	INGENIOUS	IMPLORE	CHAOS	CONTRIVED
DAUNTLESS	UNPALATABLE	COVET	INVARIABLY	CARICATURE
VAIN	MUTUAL	FREE SPACE	TEDIOUS	BLISS
PLAUSIBLE	SMOTE	ELOQUENT	COUNTENANCE	ABASHED
ODIOUS	UPBRAID	PRECARIOUS	MELANCHOLY	ALACRITY

Tom Sawyer Vocabulary

AWED	SEAR	ABSTAIN	VICE	MAGNANIMOUS
SUBDUED	AVERTED	IMPERISHABLE	PRECIPICE	PERPLEXED
ASSENT	PRODIGIOUS	FREE SPACE	CONDESCEND	OPPRESSIVE
IMPAIRED	CEASED	APPEASED	CONSENT	DISDAIN
COGITATING	PALLID	RESOLUTION	DERISION	WARY

Tom Sawyer Vocabulary

CONSENT	IMPERISHABLE	MAGNANIMOUS	RESOLUTION	INGENIOUS
PALLID	UPBRAID	ATTRITION	DISDAIN	DAUNTLESS
UNPALATABLE	INQUEST	FREE SPACE	IMPAIRED	MELANCHOLY
VICE	ASSENT	WARY	FRESCOED	ABASHED
PRECARIOUS	TYRANNY	MUTUAL	CEASED	CONTRIVED

Tom Sawyer Vocabulary

SEAR	SUBDUED	IMPLORE	SMOTE	OPPRESSIVE
TEDIOUS	PRODIGIOUS	VAIN	PRECIPICE	ELOQUENT
ALACRITY	BLISS	FREE SPACE	DERISION	SUPPLICATION
APPREHENSIVELY	APPEASED	CONDESCEND	COVET	ABSTAIN
COUNTENANCE	PERVADING	PERPLEXED	PLAUSIBLE	AVERTED

Tom Sawyer Vocabulary

COGITATING	MAGNANIMOUS	SUBDUED	ASSENT	DISDAIN
PALLID	MELANCHOLY	PLAUSIBLE	ELOQUENT	IMPERISHABLE
IMPLORE	INGENIOUS	FREE SPACE	BLISS	COVET
OPPRESSIVE	TEDIOUS	MUTUAL	CHAOS	SEAR
CEASED	INVARIABLY	COUNTENANCE	CARICATURE	WARY

Tom Sawyer Vocabulary

UPBRAID	ATTRITION	PERVADING	ODIOUS	PRECARIOUS
ALACRITY	RESOLUTION	APPREHENSIVELY	DERISION	ABSTAIN
INQUEST	CONSENT	FREE SPACE	TYRANNY	FRESCOED
AWED	ABASHED	APPEASED	VICE	CONTRIVED
SUPPLICATION	DAUNTLESS	PRECIPICE	SMOTE	PRODIGIOUS

Tom Sawyer Vocabulary

OPPRESSIVE	INVARIABLY	VAIN	DISDAIN	PERVADING
MELANCHOLY	TEDIOUS	PALLID	ELOQUENT	UPBRAID
INQUEST	SUBDUED	FREE SPACE	AWED	COVET
MAGNANIMOUS	APPEASED	APPREHENSIVELY	UNPALATABLE	CONDESCEND
COGITATING	IMPERISHABLE	SMOTE	AVERTED	SEAR

Tom Sawyer Vocabulary

ALACRITY	PERPLEXED	ASSENT	PRECIPICE	CARICATURE
BLISS	PLAUSIBLE	VICE	CONSENT	ABSTAIN
MUTUAL	FRESCOED	FREE SPACE	ABASHED	CONTRIVED
TYRANNY	IMPLORE	CEASED	WARY	INGENIOUS
ODIOUS	ATTRITION	DERISION	SUPPLICATION	RESOLUTION

Tom Sawyer Vocabulary

APPEASED	WARY	COVET	FRESCOED	ELOQUENT
DAUNTLESS	CEASED	COUNTENANCE	ABASHED	VAIN
TYRANNY	SEAR	FREE SPACE	PRODIGIOUS	SMOTE
PALLID	MELANCHOLY	SUBDUED	OPPRESSIVE	UNPALATABLE
IMPLORE	CHAOS	PRECARIOUS	DISDAIN	COGITATING

Tom Sawyer Vocabulary

IMPAIRED	SUPPLICATION	BLISS	CONSENT	DERISION
ABSTAIN	CONTRIVED	ASSENT	CONDESCEND	PERVADING
UPBRAID	PRECIPICE	FREE SPACE	TEDIOUS	ALACRITY
INVARIABLY	MAGNANIMOUS	RESOLUTION	ATTRITION	PERPLEXED
APPREHENSIVELY	INGENIOUS	ODIOUS	AWED	MUTUAL

Tom Sawyer Vocabulary

COVET	CEASED	AVERTED	APPREHENSIVELY	IMPERISHABLE
PRECIPICE	OPPRESSIVE	DISDAIN	SMOTE	PALLID
CONSENT	INQUEST	FREE SPACE	DERISION	MAGNANIMOUS
BLISS	RESOLUTION	INGENIOUS	CONTRIVED	APPEASED
COGITATING	AWED	CHAOS	MUTUAL	TYRANNY

Tom Sawyer Vocabulary

IMPLORE	CARICATURE	SUPPLICATION	PRODIGIOUS	PERVADING
ASSENT	DAUNTLESS	ALACRITY	TEDIOUS	ODIOUS
VAIN	ABASHED	FREE SPACE	UPBRAID	ATTRITION
INVARIABLY	FRESCOED	SEAR	CONDESCEND	COUNTENANCE
WARY	ABSTAIN	MELANCHOLY	IMPAIRED	PRECARIOUS

www.ingramcontent.com/pod-product-compliance
Lightning Source LLC
Chambersburg PA
CBHW081454070526
44586CB00019B/2356